Liberating
Your Magnificence

Also by Scott Peck

The Love You Deserve: 10 Keys to Perfect Love
1998

Each of us
has a unique Life Message
that no one else
can express

Liberating Your Magnificence

25 Keys
to
Loving & Healing
Yourself

Scott Peck
and
Shannon Peck

LIBERATING YOUR MAGNIFICENCE
25 KEYS TO LOVING & HEALING YOURSELF

Lifepath Publishing
P.O. Box 830, Solana Beach, CA 92075

Grateful acknowledgement is made for:
Poem "Dare to Dream" from Diana Loomans
Poem "On My Watch" by Dessa Byrd Reed

Cover by Robert Howard

Printed   01 00 99 ♥ 10 9 8 7 6 5 4 3 2 1

Publisher's Cataloging-in-Publication
(Provided by Quality Books, Inc.)

Peck, Scott.
    Liberating your magnificence : 25 keys to
loving & healing yourself / Scott Peck and Shannon
Peck. -- 1st ed.
    p. cm.
    ISBN: 0-9659976-5-0

    1. Self-esteem. 2. Self-actualization
(Psychology) 3. Self-help techniques. 4.
Spiritual healing.   I. Peck, Shannon. II.
Title.

BF697.5.S46P43 1999   158.1
                        QBI99-851

To each individual in the universe,
these pages are dedicated to
your spiritual right
to know and radiate your unique
Magnificence

Acknowledgements

We are immensely grateful for the Magnificent team of friends and supporters who reviewed this book in advance: Helice Bridges, Kathy Faller, Bob & Sharon Griswold, Jill Lesly Jones, Collier Kaler, Diana Loomans, Janet Lynn, Khanh Nguyen, Nan Tellier, and Don Trotter.

We are also grateful for Bernhard Dohrmann, founder of the powerful Free Enterprise Forum, where dreams are cherished and brought to reality, who saw our vision and empowered us to move forward, and for all those at the Forum who have encouraged and supported us.

There are very special people who made invaluable contributions to this book: Robert Howard, our patient and inspired cover designer, Collier Kaler, talented publicist and superb editor, Diana Loomans, gifted writer & contributing poet, Linda Nelson-Hieb, hair stylist & interview participant, Dessa Reed, close friend and contributing poet, and Barry Spilchuk, precious friend, heart-based workshop leader, rocket booster, & author of the beautiful foreword to this book.

Lastly, and with great humility, we are deeply grateful for all those who have expressed such love and generosity in endorsing this book.

Foreword

By Barry Spilchuk, Co-author,
A Cup of Chicken Soup for the Soul

Let me ask you a few questions:
- What will it mean to you when you start living your life to the fullest?
- What will it be like for you when you shed self-doubt and self imposed limitations?
- How will you feel when you truly start celebrating yourself and your talents to the highest levels?
- How will your life be when you honestly start Liberating your Magnificence?

Oh, one more question:
- What will it mean to your life if you *don't* do all these things?

I do not want to scare you with that last question, but I do want to make you think. Almost everyone would love to accept the joy and magnificence that life has to offer, but the reality is, sometimes we are not aware of how to have our lives be full or what is holding us back!

Congratulations on investing in yourself by DOING this book. This is a very rare book. It actually does what the title says it does, Liberate your Magnificence....with one catch...you must do the work! But that is the fun part!

Each chapter is another step in the evolution of your fullest potential.

Inside the pages of this Handbook of Self Celebration you will embrace loving strategies that will lead you to a purposeful and more joyful life.

As I read through this book and completed the simple and enriching affirmations, I found myself expanding my capacity to serve humanity. I finally released some old hurts that I thought were long gone. I shifted to a much bigger vision of how I can contribute to helping others liberate their magnificence. I also deepened my alignment with my life's purpose!

You deserve a rich, full, abundant life – full of love and joy! Scott and Shannon Peck will show you how to move from doubt to divinity, from worry to wonder and from fear to faith.

It's time to liberate your magnificence!

You deserve it!

Respectfully,

Barry Spilchuk, Co-author,
A Cup of Chicken Soup for the Soul
& Creator of the interactive, in-home couples workshop, *Let's Talk...about Relationships.*

Table of Contents

Continued on next page

Stage 3
Free Your Magnificence

Stage 4
Radiate Your Magnificence

Appendix

Liberating
Your Magnificence

What is your substance?
Is it your looks? Title? Wealth?
No!

Your substance is
The inner core of your Identity.

Each of us
has a unique Life Message
that no one else
can express.

We are not in competition with each other.
Nor can we reach our destiny
in another's way.

Your life mission
is to liberate your inner substance
– your unique Magnificence –
to bless the universe
with what you
alone are.

And
on the way,
to love and honor and liberate
the Magnificence
of all those you pass and know.

**Scott & Shannon
Peck**

Introduction

Welcome to the liberation of your Magnificence.

You can expect huge leaps forward in your life as you read this book and move through each stage of liberation. You will learn how to:

- Identify your unique Life Message (stage 1).
- Cherish the unfolding of your highest selfhood (stage 2).
- Free yourself from doubt, guilt, lack, fear, anger, time, age, rejection, and over-whelm (stage 3).
- Radiate your Magnificence in total liberation (stage 4).

There are two excellent ways to enjoy this book:

1. Fly through the chapters to get the big picture of how to liberate your Magnificence. The chapters are short and the ideas are clear.

2. Grab a pen, sink into a comfortable chair, and prepare to *experience* your new life of Magnificence. The exercises and affirmations are powerful and the Magnificence Journal will support your heart. You will be unlikely to give away your copy of this book – to anyone.

As guides and fellow travelers on the path of liberation, we'd like to introduce ourselves to you in a personal way. We are often called "The Love Team" for two reasons:

First, we feel like the happiest married couple in the universe and we are dedicated to helping others experience this joy. That's what motivated writing *The Love You Deserve: 10 Keys to Perfect Love.*

Second, we are dedicated to bringing all mankind into the heart of Love where each individual's unique worth is honored, cherished, esteemed, and empowered. That's why we wrote this book.

All of us have extraordinary Magnificence within – but we need enormous love to bring this Magnificence out of hiding and into full clarity and radiance.

We know what will happen when you open to the truths in these pages – because it happened to us:

- Your life will rapidly shift into a greater awareness of your Magnificence.
- You will discover, through the honesty and openness of our personal stories, the power of Love to liberate *your* Life Message.
- You will feel the strength of Love supporting the inner core of your being.
- You will learn powerful spiritual principles of healing.
- You will learn how to love yourself at the highest level.

**It is your
spiritual right
to know, cherish, free, & radiate
your Magnificence**

To help you prepare for the full liberation of your Magnificence, we recommend you begin with the revealing 25-question quiz: *How Liberated is Your Magnificence?*

This quiz, located in the appendix at the back of the book, will show you where you already shine – and where you can grow. It will also give you an overview of what it feels like to live in Magnificence. Each question in the quiz corresponds to a chapter in this book.

Thank you for joining us.

Let your Magnificence come forth!

***Your
Magnificence
is already within you
ready to be revealed and radiated***

Stage 1

Identify
Your
Magnificence

Chapter 1

Open Yourself to Magnificence

Magnificence

**Grandeur • Majesty • Brilliance
Richness • Abundance
Honor • Distinction • Glory
Radiance**

These are the words that define you!

Yes, you!

Not only are you Magnificent, but the entire universe is standing on tiptoes in anticipation of your arrival – in eager readiness for the full revealing of your identity.

The question is not, "Are you Magnificent?"

The liberating question is:

"*What* is your Magnificence?"

***Each of us
has a unique Life Message
that no one else
can express***

If, for any reason, you are saying to yourself, "I don't feel Magnificent" or "I'm not sure that I am Magnificent," this book will free you from these imprisoning thoughts.

Let your heart open to the Magnificence within you

It is not egotistical to think of yourself as Magnificent. It is simply the pure acknowledgment that each of us is created with a unique Life Message that no one else can express.

That is why the words "Magnificent" and "Life Message" are capitalized in this book – to remind you, every time you see these words, that your Magnificence and Life Message come from a Higher Power.

We call that Higher Power many names in this book – divine Love, God, Spirit, Source, Truth, Infinite Mind, Soul, Universe, Infinite One, Light, Consciousness, and Higher Self. You may have additional names – but they all point to identity as inherently spiritual.

And that is why you cannot shrink from your Magnificence. It's a *fact* about you! And this book is designed to bring your Magnificence into full view and radiance. None of us can hide from our spiritual identity.

- If you doubt your Magnificence, it is time to wake to your true identity.
- If you are blind to your Magnificence, it is time to see yourself through the eyes of divine Love.
- If you are struggling to define your Magnificence, it is time for revelation.

- If you are striving to liberate your Magnificence, it is time to throw off all mental limitations and move into pure Light.

Think of all the people in the world who are suffering with low self-esteem, injustice, stress, and an absence of love. Each and every one of these individuals is Magnificent, but it takes enormous love to liberate our individual and collective Magnificence. We desperately need each other's love.

So let the love in this book wash through your identity with renewal, cherishing, and honoring. Let your inner self relax and drink in the empowering new ideas that will support your rise into Magnificence – for eternity.

We have entered a whole new era of consciousness. We all feel it. Each of us is being called forth to a higher level of spiritual thinking and living. We are all being called to Magnificence.

There are no exceptions. Each of us is full of divine passion and with this passion comes a calling.

Open your heart to your Magnificence – not as a dream or hope, but as your spiritual *right*. Let Love reveal your divine song of Magnificence.

We may not know you personally, but we are already rejoicing – knowing, that as you read this book, your unique Magnificence will rise into great clarity and radiance.

> *Responding*
> *to the sacred call of Love*
> *liberates*
> *your Magnificence*

Magnificence Affirmation

Open to Magnificence

I am open
to the full revealing
of my Magnificence

I am open
to all Love, all Truth,
all spiritual Light

I am open
to all that is Magnificent
within me

I am open
to radiating my Magnificence
to the universe

Loving Yourself with Magnificence!

Here is statement #1 again from the *Liberating Your Magnificence Quiz* in the appendix.

I am open to the Magnificence within me.

What are the three most powerful things you can do to align your life with this statement?

1. _____

_____

_____

2. _____

_____

_____

3. _____

_____

_____

It is your
spiritual right
to know yourself
as
Magnificent

Magnificence Journal

In the depth of your innermost heart and spiritual intuition, what is Love saying to you about your Magnificence?

_____

_____

_____

_____

_____

_____

_____

_____

_____

_____

_____

_____

_____

Chapter 2

Discover
the Substance of
Your Magnificence

Substance – not *form.*

Those words have the power to liberate your Magnificence like a rocket propelling you to new galaxies of insight.

> **To
> liberate
> your Magnificence,
> it is crucial to
> see your life
> in terms of substance,
> not form**

Here, for example, are the *forms* that would describe Scott's life: reporter, counselor, educator, copywriter, advertising manager, real estate broker, workshop leader, author, and speaker.

But what does that tell you about his *substance?*

- Do you know what makes him unique?
- Do those titles reveal his Magnificence or
  Life Message?

No!

All those jobs, occupations, positions, titles, and activities are simply *forms* – ways that he has been expressed. They do not reveal his *substance* – the meaning of his life, his unique Life Message, his Magnificence.

We can look at any person's life in the same way.

At different points throughout Shannon's life, her *form* would have been labeled: airline attendant, customer relations trainer, hotel sales manager, TV talk show host, wife, mother, ministerial council member, prison chaplain, spiritual healer, author, and speaker.

But these *forms* do not reveal Shannon's *substance*, her unique Life Message and Magnificence.

We all must climb out of the clutter of *form* to get to our Magnificence.

- Are you a mother, father, husband, wife, son, daughter?   That is the *form* of your life, not your substance.

- Are you single, divorced, or married? That too is simply the present *form* of your life, not your substance.

- Do you have a job, an occupation, a title, a position, a salary, and tasks? Those too are the *forms* of your life, not your substance.

- Are you young, old, White, Black, Hispanic, Asian? These only describe your *form*, not your substance.

> *The liberation*
> *of our Magnificence*
> *begins*
> *when we look at our lives*
> *through the lens of substance*
> *rather than*
> *form*

To see the substance of our Life Message, we must rise above the forms of our lives.

Let's look at your life now and separate *form* from *substance*.

List five *forms* – ways – in which your life has been expressed – titles, occupations, activities, events, roles, relationships:

1. _____

2. _____

3. _____

4. _____

5. _____

**The forms
of your life only hint at
the substance of your Magnificence**

Now, name three moments in your life when you felt your true *substance* was most fully expressed. Put those moments in the left column. Then ask yourself, "What were the qualities I was expressing right then?" Put those qualities in the right column.

Moments	Qualities
1. _____	_____
_____	_____
_____	_____
_____	_____
2. _____	_____
_____	_____
_____	_____
_____	_____
_____	_____
3. _____	_____
_____	_____
_____	_____
_____	_____

As you focus on the qualities that best describe you, your *substance* becomes more apparent. We are getting closer and closer to your Magnificence.

**The qualities you express
at your
highest life moments
reveal the substance
of your
Magnificence**

Your
"Magnificent Name"

Here is a fun exercise that will reveal the true substance of your Magnificence.

At our workshops on *Liberating Your Magnificence*, we ask participants to describe the *substance* of who they are in only two words.

Here are some of the Magnificent names participants have given themselves:

- Purity & Joy
- Clarity & Supporter
- Generosity & Teacher
- Spiritual & Healer
- Enthusiastic & Teacher
- Honest & Sensitive
- Ebullient & Love

How's that for revealing *substance!*

As they got in the swing of thinking of their *substance* in this new way, they began to introduce themselves to each other with their new Magnificent names: "Pure Joy," "Clear Supporter," "Generous Teacher," "Spiritual Healer," "Enthusiastic Teacher," "Honest Sensitivity," and "Ebullient Love."

These inspired names broke free of *form* and enabled these participants to align themselves with their true *substance* and Magnificence.

Now it's your turn.

Use the space below to list potential words for your new two-word Magnificent name. Remember, you can change your name anytime you wish – for eternity.

Which two words best describe the *substance* of who you are?

1. _____

2. _____

┌─────────────────────────────────────┐
│   So, my Magnificent name is   │
│   │
│ _____   _____ │
│   │
└─────────────────────────────────────┘

Every time
you practice your Magnificent name,
the substance of your identity
becomes clearer – to you!

Magnificence Affirmation

Substance,
not Form

*My true substance
can never be measured
by the forms
of my life*

*I see
that the qualities
that best define me
reveal the true substance
of my life*

*I listen
with humility & joy
as infinite Love
opens me to the discovery of
my Magnificence*

Loving Yourself with Magnificence!

Here is statement #2 again from the *Liberating Your Magnificence Quiz* in the appendix.

**I understand that my Magnificence
is the *substance* of who I am,
not the *form* of my life (job, title, role).**

What are the three most powerful things you can do to align your life with this statement?

1. _____
   _____
   _____

2. _____
   _____
   _____

3. _____
   _____
   _____

*It is your
spiritual right
to know the substance
of your identity*

Magnificence Journal

What are you discovering about your *substance*?

_____

_____

_____

_____

_____

_____

_____

_____

_____

_____

_____

_____

_____

_____

Chapter 3

Clarify
Your
Unique Life Message

You have a unique Life Message – a message so Magnificent that the universe is demanding that you come forth.

Your Life Message is the essence of who you are – the highest gift within you to be contributed to the universe. In short, your life work.

Are you ready to summarize your Life Message in one sentence? You will do just that by the end of this chapter – and you will be amazed at how much clarity this will give you.

Imagine Love calling to you, inviting you to know your Magnificence, whispering these words:

It is your
spiritual right
to know your Magnificence
so clearly
that your whole life
resonates with spiritual clarity

As you enter this sacred space of Love, let all egotism dissolve. Step out of any restricted thinking about yourself to the embrace of infinite Love that knows your true, *infinite* nature.

We're going to start this journey in a hair salon.

A Lesson in Magnificence
at the Hair Salon

As we were working on this chapter, we both stopped in for a haircut – from Linda, who we love as much for her reliable cut as for her joy.

With a smile and hello, we instantly jumped into questions – to learn more about her Magnificence.

"Linda, what are the words that best describe who you truly are?"

With her characteristic warmth and openness, Linda immediately joined the adventure. Here were her words:

- Joyful
- Enthusiastic
- Peace-loving
- Soothing
- Nurturing
- Creative
- Loving
- Giving
- Generous

These words flowed from Linda with almost complete effortlessness and delight. We were both charmed by what she was identifying as her *substance*.

We continued:

"What one word is still missing in describing who you truly are?"

She answered immediately:

- Spirituality

With joy and appreciation of her great openness, we continued:

"At the depth of your being, Linda, what is your passion?"

She answered with a smile and great clarity:

"Art and bringing beauty to others."

As she said these words, we thought of how much art and beauty she contributed right here in the hair salon – her creative jewelry, her loving enthusiasm, her freedom of thought, her happy discussions of her stained-glass artwork.

"Linda, what do you think will be the effect of your life?"

"I want to enrich people's lives – to contribute something of lasting value and beauty – to bring joy to people."

What Magnificence!

Here we were in the middle of a busy salon, talking to a "hair stylist."   But look how much more was revealed when we rose above the *form*. Behind the *form* called "hair stylist" was the *substance* of Linda – full of joy, creativity, soul, and a great desire to bring art and beauty to mankind.

*Your
Magnificence
is not your title or job
but the substance
of your being*

Another One-of-a-Kind Example

It's not always so easy to gather your Magnificence into such instant clarity as Linda did.

We can't imagine a better way to help you learn the creative process of identifying your unique Life Message than letting you sit in on a breakfast Scott had with our friend Don Trotter.

Don is passionate about many things – organic gardening, the environment, science, research, writing, creativity, and love. One never knows what's next with Don. Even Don!

For example, he recently purchased land in Nevada and started a mining operation for fossilized kelp – which he named Kelzyme. He has already shipped tons of Kelzyme worldwide to help reclaim forests and soils. Don also writes entertaining and informative organic gardening columns.

So it was with relish that Scott asked Don a series of questions about his Life Message:

"Don, what are the 10 words that best describe what is most special about you? Don't hold back. Don't be modest. Speak to me with truth."

Don looked into space with a twinkle and began:

- "Enthusiasm!"
- "Generosity of spirit!"
- "Laughter – lots of laughter! Being humorous wherever I go."
- "Clear vision of the natural world outside of Science-speak."
- "Connected to nature and the natural beauty of other human beings."

He paused.   Scott stayed silent – encouraging him with unconditional love to reveal his whole heart. He continued:

- "Hunger for knowledge."
- "Sharp mind."
- "Appreciation for the dreams of others and being supportive of them."
- "Natural teacher."

"Wow!" Scott conveyed, appreciating his honesty and open heart. "That's nine. Want to try for ten?"

- "OK, I'm a really, really lousy driver – really, I am!"

We laughed and I asked a second question:

"Don, how would you summarize your Life Message in 10 words or less – what you most want to contribute to the universe?"

Don took a short breath – and out spilled this 214 word-burst of energy:

"One of the things that separates us from other beings is aesthetics – our ability to appreciate beauty. So many people have the capacity to accept beauty on the surface but there's so much more to see.

Yes, a tree can be beautiful and a human being and an animal can be beautiful, but if you put them into their natural habitat where they feel like they belong, they become even more beautiful.

A case in point, you and Shannon in your home. You created an environment there you love – and you two are beautiful there.   Not that you are not beautiful everywhere else, but you're more beautiful in that environment because it's so special – it's your home, your touchstone.

For a MaCaw parrot, home is the South American jungle. For a mountain gorilla, home is the highlands of Uganda or somewhere similar.

These animals thrive in these conditions. Yet we have a tendency to relate these animals to a zoo – and that's not where they came from.

Part of my message is accepting the beauty of nature as nature made it. Basically, I guess, my Life Message would be to help the general public become as aware of the natural beauty of Earth as we should – and can. How's that for a short answer?"

This was Don's first attempt to summarize his Life Message in 10 words or less. We were both laughing at his lengthy reply! Yet the inner, Magnificent Don was emerging from the forest of words.

"What caused you to respond so openly Don?" asked Scott.

"If you had asked me this question ten years ago, I wouldn't have been able to tell you anything. My Life Message then was basically to scream at people all over the world and move trees (he laughed). We evolve. I'm now able to get more in touch with the person that lies inside. The tree mover, gardener, writer – these are things I do, not who I am." (note: *form*, not *substance*.)

"Don, what caused you to move past that identity of being a screaming tree mover?"

"Well, basically that screaming tree person got way too tired of screaming. I always knew a flame was burning within me. I just never knew how to get to it. But as I grew older, the flame was just undeniable. And now here it is."

"Why did it take so long to recognize your life flame?"

"Because I was concentrating on work and earning lots of money. I watched sports, traveled a lot, and made lots of money. The point is... I had no life! I was making money, but I wasn't really living."

"Don, what do you hope will be the effect of your Life Message?"

"The hoped-for effect would certainly be that we, as a society – and globally – learn to appreciate the amazing diversity of life on this planet. That includes the diversity of ethnic differences that we as human beings share as well as the diversity of minerals, animals, and plants.

We don't need to go hug a tree, but we can appreciate its existence and honor its space without thinking, 'Oh boy, that will make a great fire.' And in the same way, to honor people. It is the differences in our ethnic diversity that make us such a rich society."

"OK Don, are you ready to try for a one-sentence summary of your Life Message?"

Don's eyes sparkled with the challenge.

"To help human beings become more aware of the beauty and diversity around them – that our whole planet is a rare and beautiful place and so are its inhabitants."

Even though
it may require a thousand words
or awkward silent moments,
love yourself
enough to let
your Magnificence
emerge into
Light

How to Pull a Life Message
Out of Hiding

Look how clearly we can see into Don's being – Don's Magnificence. The real Don is not a miner, researcher, writer, gardener. That is his *form.*

The real Don is passionate about diversity and beauty. This is his *substance* – the music of his heart.

So what can we learn about identifying one's Life Message from this breakfast with Don and our haircut with Linda:

- It takes an environment of trust, openness, no judgment, and un-conditional love for a Life Message to come out of its shell with another person.

- It sometimes takes a lot of words to get at the inner truth of our unique Life Message – even for ourselves.

- Magnificence cannot be described in terms of one's current job or activities. To see our Magnificence, we must penetrate beyond the events of our life to the soul being expressed.

- It helps a great deal to laugh during the process – a lot! Humor opens new doors.

- And, as Don said, "The tree mover, gardener, writer – these are things I do, not who I am. When you get down to who you are and accept that, there's a beautiful message there."

Please Join us for Breakfast

Let's suppose that you – right now – are sitting with us in a quiet booth having a leisurely breakfast.

Imagine too that we have come together with great love and honoring for each other – with the goal of identifying each other's unique Life Message.

We can't wait to ask you the same questions we asked Linda and Don, but our inner voice is telling us that you might feel more comfortable and free – and be even more prepared – if we went first.

"OK Scott & Shannon," you graciously ask, "what are the 10 words that best describe what is most special about each of you?"

With a bold decision to be totally honest, here is our reply:

Shannon	Scott
1. Loving	1. Compassion
2. Healing	2. Empathy
3. Nurturing	3. Universal love
4. Enthusiasm	4. Unconditional love
5. Inspiring	5. Spirituality
6. Divine viewpoint	6. Kindness
7. Creative	7. Empowering
8. Principled	8. Teacher of hearts
9. Spiritual growth	9. Love of mentoring
10. Advancing others	10. Peacemaker

"Wow!" we think, "That feels good. Those really are the words of our Magnificence. This is what the entire universe is gaining – from *us*!"

"OK, how would you two summarize your Life Message – what you most want to contribute to the universe?"

Shannon answers first:

"I want to drastically lessen suffering, tears, emotional pain, and arguing in the world. My desire is to awaken massive global love that pours forth where people are inspired to love more and are daily focused on love. I want to contribute to a world where all life's possibilities are seen to be accomplished by loving more – where we all live in a consciousness of love that heals our bodies, relationships, communities, and life directions. That's my goal!"

Scott answers:

"Thank you for asking. This question forces me to think BIG – to step out of false humility or ego into divine space. It's taken me years to look at myself in the mirror of Soul and see Magnificence, but here is what I see as I truly love myself:

I feel within me an enormous desire to love all mankind. This is such a strong message within me that it has the force of divinity announcing its pure nature through my inner being. I am dedicated to helping people feel Love's unconditional embrace – to feel upheld, uplifted, empowered, and liberated to be all they are gifted to be."

"Shannon, what do you hope will be the effect of your Life Message?"

"I see the effect of my life message as:

- Hearts awakened to the divine.
- A global vision of spiritual power used for healing ourselves and others.
- More love for each other – everywhere.
- Great joy & happiness & empowerment globally.

- Sharing, caring, laughter.
- Tremendous life enhancement.

"Scott, what do you hope will be the effect of your Life Message?"

"I see the effect of my Life Message as raising the consciousness of world thought to the understanding that we can and must love and honor each other – and that this is not only achievable, but practical. I hope that my life will contribute to empowering individuals and mankind to learn the tangible ways that Love can be expressed to each other."

"OK you two, can you summarize your Life Message in one sentence?"

Shannon goes first:

"My highest desire is to express the allness and oneness of God through the power of divine Love and healing."

Adds Scott:

"I have to be honest here. Getting married to Shannon was an enormous turning point in clarity for me. We both felt our Life Messages unite in Spirit when we came together.

We knew we wanted to help people learn more about Love, but Love itself forced us to move even higher than that. We took the mental leap into God's view of our Magnificence and arrived at the words of our life mission statement together:

Bringing all mankind into the heart of Love.

That's our Life Message. Shannon is passionate about spiritual healing and I'm passionate about Love. But what's the real difference? Healing brings us to the heart of Love. And Love heals."

It's Time for
Your Magnificence

The moment has arrived to learn about *your* Magnificence!

We hope you will open your heart with us. There are no wrong answers. We know that within you lies enormous Magnificence and we are already loving you unconditionally.

As we ask you the same questions that we asked Linda and Don and that you asked us, use the open spaces to write or jot down your thoughts.

Our first question to you is on the next page.

"What are the 10 words that best describe what is most special about you? Don't hold back. Don't be modest. Speak to us with truth."

1. _____

2. _____

3. _____

4. _____

5. _____

6. _____

7. _____

8. _____

9. _____

10._____

These
are the words
of your Magnificence.
This is what the entire universe
is blessed to be receiving – from you!

"How would you describe your Life Message – the highest gift you have to contribute to the universe?" Use the whole page and let your heart ramble into clarity."

To cherish
the tender shoots
of your unique Magnificence
is a
divine act
of loving yourself

"What do you hope will be the effect of your Life Message?" Don't hold back. Let your deepest passions loose."

*This is the
effect
– the grandeur and scope –
of your
Magnificent identity
rippling out
to the
entire universe*

"OK, here's the last question. How would you summarize your Life Message in one sentence?"

You are totally free to change your answer throughout eternity, so use this opportunity to love yourself and share your very best at this moment of your Magnificence.

My Life Message in one sentence:

Now that is what we call a Magnificent breakfast! Sharing dreams and listening to each other strengthens each of us.

When we
unite
in shining the light
on each other's unique identity
we enable each other
to rise
to the truth
of our
Magnificence

Magnificence Affirmation

Magnificence Within

As I look into Mind,
I see myself
as Mind sees me –
infinite, majestic, unique

As I look into Soul,
I see myself
as Soul sees me –
radiant, beautiful, Soulful

As I look into Love,
I see myself
as Love sees me –
generous, compassionate, loving

As I commune with God,
I know myself
as I am –
spiritual, at one with Soul,
Magnificent

Loving Yourself with Magnificence!

Here is statement #3 again from the *Liberating Your Magnificence Quiz* in the appendix.

I am able to identify my unique Life Message in one sentence.

What are the three most powerful things you can do to align your life with this statement?

1. _____
   _____
   _____

2. _____
   _____
   _____

3. _____
   _____
   _____

*It is your
spiritual right
to know
your Life Message
with clarity*

Magnificence Journal

What have you discovered about your unique Life Message?

_____

_____

_____

_____

_____

_____

_____

_____

_____

_____

_____

_____

_____

_____

Stage 2

Cherish
Your
Magnificence

Chapter 4

Gift
Yourself
with
Sacred Solitude

Your Magnificence is as precious as a newborn child.

And this child is *you!*

The most loving care you can give to yourself as your Magnificence begins its journey into Light is to gift yourself with sacred solitude.

What is sacred solitude?

It is loving yourself enough to retreat from the world's mental forces in order to protect the emergence and strengthening of your true self and Magnificence.

Even as we write this chapter to you, we are sitting in the sacred solitude of a tiny office that few even know exists. It was our gift to each other to bring forth this book in the stillness of Soul. Writing this book is all that happens in this sacred space.

Truth
becomes
visible to thought
in
utter
stillness

Don't miss the point here. Having a secret office isn't the message.

The message is to gift yourself with solitude that is sacred – where you can be alone with yourself and quietly cherish your emerging Magnificence.

For example, you can:

- Drive or walk to a nearby park and sit alone in the sacred silence of nature. Open yourself to the natural calm within.

- Turn off the TV, radio, and phones in your home for an hour of sacred contemplation. Experience the stillness.

- Drop your kids off at their next event and then drive around the corner to a quiet spot and allow yourself to experience total reverence of your Magnificence.

- When you go on your next errand to the supermarket, include a dip into sacred solitude while you sit in your car. Accept the fullness of this moment.

All this, of course, is possible.

But it won't happen unless you care for your newborn Magnificence as a mother cares for her new infant. A new child needs nurturing, attention, and unconditional love.

Your Magnificence is no less important.

> *Treat yourself*
> *to the nurturing, attention,*
> *and unconditional love*
> *that your*
> *Magnificence*
> *deserves*

If your boss at work wanted to discuss a promotion for you, would you agree to meet?

Of course! Well, with all due respect:

Liberating
your *Magnificence*
is the
biggest promotion
you will
ever receive – in eternity

Shannon is a master of using sacred solitude in her healing work.

Here are her own words:

———————

Some of my most gratifying and powerful moments occur each day in my quiet time.

This has been a habit in all my years of spiritual healing work. I am so dependent on this period of quietness that if I don't receive it, I feel spiritually wobbly until I take the time.

My sacred solitude usually lasts about an hour – and sometimes longer. You may not have a full hour, but time is not the issue. Consistency with sacred solitude is everything.

My morning meditation is usually directed towards solving specific problems. This is where I pull out my entire list of what needs to be healed – within myself, with family members, and with those who have asked for help.

I roll up my spiritual sleeves in sacred stillness and go for healing results. I use denials and affirmations, intuition, guidance, and loads of love.

It's a time of listening to divine thoughts and letting these unfoldments lift me to a view of Magnificence wherever I mentally look.

For example, if I'm working to help someone with low self-esteem, I deny worthlessness as having any part of identity. I also deny self-doubt, fear, parental conditioning, being a victim of blame or accusation, feeling unloved, or a lack of appreciation.

I label these as the specific thoughts comprising the belief called low self-esteem. I remind myself that this is not a reality, but a false perception – a set of *thoughts* rather than a real *condition.*

Then, in sacred stillness, I switch to affirmations and I think of the person's spirituality and divine origin. I affirm his or her exemption from the belief of low self-esteem. I spend time loving the person and seeing his or her state of true love, value, necessity to all life, confidence, assurance, comfort, peace, perfection, and wholeness.

I remind myself that our divine origin means that each of us, in Truth, has been parented by divine Love. Our background is written by Love's hand, and this is the whole of our history.

I quietly love the person's Magnificence and see all creation expressing gratitude for what he or she truly represents.

***Sacred solitude
brings forth a flood of
inspiration
&
healing thoughts***

At other times during the day, I use moments of solitude to pray for guidance and to gather new energy and inspiration.

I am often led to think globally of all the people yearning to live in safety, love, and the freedom to express their Magnificence. I envision divine Love protecting, encouraging, and praising them.

These daily moments of sacred solitude are enormously healing. The divine guidance that unfolds during these times – when each of us is quiet and listening – unifies the universe.

Our mutually unfolding Truth-thoughts are like armies of angels going forth to heal and triumph on every mission.

During those moments of sacred solitude, I feel that I am walking around in the consciousness of infinite Love. And I see everyone else as the consciousness of Love. We are one. Stillness allows us to see that our hearts are united.

Imagine how many people in the world are praying in just this way even as you read this book. Let us thank them now, and thank everyone who has ever prayed for the world. Our united prayers are a divine force that propels us all forward to Magnificence.

In sacred solitude, we unite with all mankind.

In sacred solitude
our unity
emerges in consciousness
and the entire world
is
uplifted

Listen
in Sacred Solitude
to Your Magnificence

Go to a quiet place where you can be alone with yourself – totally undisturbed.

Allow yourself to forget all that is taking place in your life. Let there be stillness in your thinking – no judgment of yourself or anyone else. Let go of what all others think about you and how that affects you.

Let your heart open to its most reverent and highest place. Quietly accept into your thinking only thoughts that come to you directly from your Higher Self – your spiritual intuition.

In the quietness of sacred stillness, your spiritual intuition will surface and point you closer to the heart of your Magnificence.

Let yourself feel the presence of infinite Love speaking in your heart the following truth:

Yes!
You are
Magnificent
and I am even now
guiding you
forward
to full awareness and liberation

Magnificence Affirmation
Sacred Solitude

*All alone
with Love
I open my thought in
sacred solitude*

*I listen
and accept
the soft nurturing
of Soul*

*I accept
Love's revealing of
my Magnificence*

*I cherish Love's Magnificent
expression of each
individual
in the universe*

Loving Yourself with Magnificence!

Here is statement #4 again from the *Liberating Your Magnificence Quiz* in the appendix.

I give myself sacred solitude
to nurture and cherish my
Magnificence.

What are the three most powerful things you can do to align your life with this statement?

1. _____

   _____

   _____

2. _____

   _____

   _____

3. _____

   _____

   _____

*It is your
spiritual right
to know & experience
sacred solitude*

Magnificence Journal

In the sacred stillness of your own solitude, what new views of your Magnificence are emerging?

_____

_____

_____

_____

_____

_____

_____

_____

_____

_____

_____

_____

_____

_____

Chapter 5

See Yourself
As Already
Whole

You are *whole – complete* – right now!

That is the underlying truth of your being – your real identity.

Yet as soon as this spiritual truth is uttered, we are assaulted with self-thoughts that say we are *incomplete* – that we are missing *something* important before we can be whole:

- A love-mate.
- A job that satisfies.
- Time to follow our passion.
- Enough money to live outside of pressure.
- Freedom from an overload of tasks and responsibilities.
- The completion of a major project.

How many times per day do thoughts like these attack your wholeness?

Thoughts of incompleteness truly are attacks – assaults on your identity! They are as damaging as if a rocket exploded in your house – but the rocket, in this case, is constant *mental* bombardment, and the house is your consciousness.

To liberate our Magnificence, our task is to slice through this fog of burdening, oppressive *thinking* to new mental ground.

It is your spiritual right
to see yourself
as whole

This powerful statement of Truth declares war on thoughts barraging us with inadequacy and incompleteness. This is our spiritual defense against all attacks on our wholeness, identity, and Magnificence. And here is the good news:

We
always go forward
when we
stay anchored
in our
spirituality

We often ask our audiences at talks or workshops, "How many of you consider yourselves to be spiritually-minded?"

Whether we are in California, Illinois, Georgia, or New York, more than 95% of all hands rise when we ask this question – clear evidence of expanding spiritual consciousness that is transforming us all.

We are all being compelled to transcend old modes of thinking – and not to *think* about it, but to *do* it!

The time has come,
not to dabble in spirituality,
but to
become experts
in declaring and defending
our
spiritual wholeness

We become experts in defending our wholeness by spiritual reasoning that transcends what appear to be conditions.

***The enemy
to our completeness
is never a condition,
but a mental attack on our
spiritual identity***

Here is an example from Scott's life – in his own words:

———————

After my previous marriage ended in divorce, I felt unworthy and unlovable.

In a nutshell, my condition seemed to be:

- Divorced.
- Without self-esteem.
- Stuck in a job that wasn't me.
- Without much hope.

Can you imagine how many thousands of times these thoughts attacked my identity and worth?

Yet one day, in the very midst of these conditions that seemed so real, my spiritual consciousness cut through these thought-attacks to a higher reality. My spiritual intuition took the floor and declared:

"You, Scott, deserve to receive as much love as you give. In fact, you deserve to be loved *perfectly* – to experience a marriage anchored in divine Love. And Scott, this is your spiritual *right!*"

This spiritual insight shocked me, but two seconds later, I realized,

"Yes! This is the truth. This is divine Love speaking to me directly about my nature as Love's own expression. I am at one with Love and it is spiritually natural for me – as Love's expression – to experience all of Love. Yes, it *is* my spiritual *right* to experience perfect love."

In that moment of spiritual listening and reasoning, my entire consciousness was transformed – even though conditions in my life had not changed.

My new spiritual consciousness opened my thought to receive love at a level I had never imagined possible before. It was no accident that Shannon soon entered my life – my best friend, wife, and spiritual partner.

One wonderful result of our marriage was writing the book, *The Love You Deserve*, written to help others claim their spiritual right to this same love. And you are now reading our first co-authored book – on Magnificence!

What extraordinary results – all from a change of consciousness!

Do you get the point?

I didn't set out to change my *conditions*.

What changed the *conditions* in my life was a change in my spiritual *consciousness*.

What happened to me was not magic or manipulation. I simply rose to the consciousness of my inherent spirituality.

This is what can happen to you. This same spiritual freedom is *already* yours.

***We are in a revolution
that is challenging & empowering
us to see our spirituality
as real***

Here are some powerful truths about your wholeness:

Your wholeness
means
that you are
incapable of any loss – forever

Incapable of loss!

Think of it. This is just the opposite of *thoughts* that tell us we are suffering from loss. We only *believe* we are capable of losing our health, mind, love, job, children, money, keys – you name it.

The spiritual reality of our lives, however, is wholeness, not loss. Spiritual consciousness brings us into alignment with wholeness.

Your
wholeness is
incapable of being separated
from all good – forever

Inseparable from all good!

Imagine being guaranteed that you could never be separated from security, safety, harmony, love, joy, peace, and power. This is the truth of your spiritual status.

Your
wholeness
is indivisible

Spirit's wholeness is inherent.

Think of an image in a hologram prism. If you dropped the prism and it broke into a thousand pieces, each piece would still contain the whole image. The image cannot be divided.

This is the spiritual picture of your wholeness. This may seem like an entirely new way of thinking, but your identity is not in need of putting pieces back together.

***You are
inherently and already
whole***

The more you flex your spiritual muscle and see yourself as whole, the more powerful you will become and the more whole you will feel.

What matters most is that we choose spiritual weapons to defeat the attacks on our identity. That is why this book is so loaded with affirmations. These pure statements of Love and Truth enable us to become experts in spiritual reasoning – to align our lives with spiritual Light.

***When we
open to the core
of our innate wholeness,
we align ourselves with
divine Light
that liberates
our Magnificence***

Hired as a
Spiritual Defense Attorney

Situation: You are under attack by mental forces that are suggesting (as your own thought): "I am incomplete and here is the evidence – I am alone, fearful, and full of doubt about my future."

Exercise: Assume that you have just been retained to be the spiritual **defense** attorney against these mental attacks. Write below the three strongest statements of spiritual truth about your wholeness that will guarantee your victory:

1. _____

   _____

2. _____

   _____

3. _____

   _____

Your wholeness is infinite
Nothing can be added
Nothing can be subtracted
You are complete
right now

Magnificence Affirmation
I am whole

I listen
with an open heart
to
Truth's song about me
called
"My Magnificence"

I hear
the words
of Love's song for me pour forth the
message of pure Love
"I am whole!"

From the
core of my being
I acknowledge
and
cherish
my completeness

Loving Yourself with Magnificence!

Here is statement #5 again from the *Liberating Your Magnificence Quiz* in the appendix.

I see myself as *already* whole, not incomplete.

What are the three most powerful things you can do to align your life with this statement?

1. _____
   _____
   _____

2. _____
   _____
   _____

3. _____
   _____
   _____

*It is your
spiritual right
to know yourself as
whole*

Magnificence Journal

As you listen to your deepest spiritual intuition, what are you learning about your wholeness?

Chapter 6

Refuse
To Compare Yourself
With Others

Are you ready for a gigantic step forward in liberating your Magnificence?

Here are three statements with enough raw spiritual energy to lift you into instantaneous Light:

You are unique!
No one else can take your place.
You are not in competition.

These statements have enormous liberating power.

For example, early in Scott's promotion of *The Love You Deserve*, there were times when he walked into a major bookstore to give a scheduled talk and felt overwhelmed with insignificance.

The attack on his self-worth came with these internal thoughts:

"Here I am surrounded by over 100,000 other books and authors – and look at all these best-sellers and all the new books!

- Who am I?
- Do I really have anything of value to contribute?
- How can I possibly compete with all these authors and books?"

This, of course, was a giant *mental* attack on his identity – on his unique substance – but it felt very real.

At times like this, Scott found a private spot in the bookstore or coffee shop and immediately tuned in deeply to his core spiritual being. Some of his very best prayers and spiritual insights came from these moments alone on the "author tour" road.

Here is an example of how he privately reasoned as he prepared for a book talk:

"I am not here in this bookstore to compete with any of these authors. I am here to express love so richly that anybody in my presence will feel uplifted – will feel embraced by Love itself.

Divine Love directed me, with Shannon's enormous support, to write *The Love You Deserve* and I trust that same supreme power of Love to express me in Love's highest way right here in this bookstore. Even if only one person comes tonight and walks away with a higher consciousness of what is possible in love, I will have been true to my inner Life Message.

Furthermore, I affirm that that there is an abundance of room in the universe for each and every writer's message to be received and loved. We are not competing with each other. We are each expressing infinite, uncontainable Soul in our unique ways – and each of these ways is of great value.

I see myself, not just someone sitting in a bookstore, but standing in the universe of infinite Mind, observing and cherishing Mind as it sends its beautiful and empowering message through all the universe, using each of us as unique and needed messengers."

When Scott reasoned spiritually this way, he felt a wave of deep peace throughout his being. He found himself re-anchored in his *substance* – to bring love to all mankind.

Can you see how he stepped out of the *form* of a "booktalk" into the *substance* of his Life Message? Not surprisingly, his booktalks were very successful – attracting many to the message of Love.

Success was not measured by how many people came or how many books were sold. The real measure of success was how *substance-anchored* he was – how much he was reaching people with his Life Message of unconditional love.

Magnificence consciousness constantly rejects the smallness of thinking about *form* and moves us to the grand *substance* of our highest identity.

> **No one**
> **else can take your place**
> **in eternity**
> **No one!**
> **You are not**
> **in competition**

Remember, too, no one else can protect your identity as forcefully as you.

We're talking *internal* security!

Think of yourself as protecting your own uniqueness as intelligently and forcefully as a top-level security guard on duty to protect the President. That is how important your unique Life Message is to the universe!

As we become more alert to our internal security needs, we become experts at identifying intruder thoughts in our private consciousness such as the following comparison thoughts:

- Will I ever be as rich as...?
- Am I as smart as...?
- Will I ever be as loved as...?
- I wish I had the opportunities that she or he...
- I might as well give up. I can never do it as well as...
- Look how much better I am than...
- Am I as good looking as...?
- I wonder if I'll ever be as successful as...?

Become aware that such thoughts are attacks on your identity, your uniqueness, your spirituality, and your Magnificence.

Defend yourself against every such mental attack on your identity. Remember these truths:

**We are not in competition with each other
nor can we reach our destiny
in another's way**

**Your life mission
is to liberate your inner substance
– your unique Magnificence –
to bless the universe
with what you
alone are**

Magnificence Affirmation

Unique & United

*I acknowledge
infinite Mind
as the Source of all substance,
all identity,
all uniqueness*

*In deep
humility & reverence
I acknowledge my oneness
with infinite Mind.*

*I see that
we are all united in Spirit
yet each
totally unique*

*I cherish
unique Magnificence for myself
and all mankind*

Loving Yourself with Magnificence!

Here is statement #6 again from the *Liberating Your Magnificence Quiz* in the appendix.

I refuse to compare myself with others.

What are the three most powerful things you can do to align your life with this statement?

1. _____

   _____

   _____

2. _____

   _____

   _____

3. _____

   _____

   _____

It is your
spiritual right
to know yourself as
unique

Magnificence Journal

In the privacy of your unique identity, what are you discovering as the truth about comparisons?

_____

_____

_____

_____

_____

_____

_____

_____

_____

_____

_____

_____

_____

_____

Chapter 7

Surround Yourself With People Who Honor You

You deserve to be surrounded by people who:

Cherish
who you are

Honor
your identity

Esteem
your Magnificence

Empower
you to expand into all possibilities

*When we
surround ourselves
with people who
cherish, honor, esteem, & empower us,
we liberate the Magnificence
we were appointed
to share
with the Universe*

To be surrounded by people who honor you is not just a happy thought or desire. It is your spiritual *right* to be deeply valued and this is the natural outcome of the *principle of honoring.*

Here is a good example of the power of this principle of honoring from Scott's life – in his words:

A number of years ago, as a full-time real estate broker, I took stock of my clients. Most were wonderful. But a few made life very difficult.

Even just a few people in your life who are questioning your motives, your value, or your skills can unnerve your joy and depress your expression of Magnificence.

Well, I made a huge decision. I decided to follow the principle of honoring – that I deserved to be associated with friends as well as business associates who expressed respect and valuing of me. I decided that I would seek out only clients who truly valued what I had to offer.

Despite knowing in my heart that I deserved this, I had some doubts about this strategy financially. Would this cause a big drop in income?

Shannon encouraged and honored my decision. And because of her spiritual awareness of the power of the principle of honoring, she knew the outcome in advance! She understood the universal truth that none of us need suffer penalties for negative behaviors and attitudes from others who have not yet done their own inner, spiritual cleansing work.

The results of my decision were extraordinary. One year later, I had served half the number of clients, doubled my income, and become a top-performing Prudential agent nationwide.

But the BIG news was this:

Because I worked only with those clients who were attracted to my qualities and who showed their appreciation of me, my clients became friends. The elimination of even those few clients that had previously drained my self-worth freed me to soar.

I found myself surrounded by clients whose love showed itself in mutual respect and support, honesty, kindness, fairness, and unselfishness. It was liberating to surround myself with these qualities.

And that wasn't all!

This dramatic change in the *mental* climate of my life did even more. Because I felt so liberated to be myself – and so valued by those around me – I was energized to express even more of my individuality and *substance* and, during the very same year, wrote *The Love You Deserve* with Shannon's powerful help.

How's that for the principle of honoring?

What began as a simple business strategy following the principle of honoring became a strategy that also liberated my Magnificence.

———————

This is exactly what *you* deserve.

Most of us are not free to select our clients, boss, or associates. But, too often, we let people who do not honor us have great influence in our lives.

Allow this principle of honoring to enter your life gently. It is not a question of eliminating people from your life. It is a question of acknowledging your own worth and moving to surround yourself with people who support your worth, identity, and Magnificence.

The goal is to liberate your Magnificence. The goal is also for you to love others and support the liberation of their Magnificence.

Here is a revealing exercise. The next time you are at lunch with a friend, privately ask yourself these questions:

- Do I feel cherished, honored, esteemed, & empowered by this person?
- Does he or she feel cherished, honored, esteemed, & empowered by me?
- Is there an equality of sharing or is one of us dominating and the other subordinate?
- Is my heart being listened to? Am I truly listening myself?

These are penetrating questions – and they instantly give illuminating answers. You will quickly see the quality of your relationships and how much honoring they do – or do not – contain.

Unfortunately, those who dominate – out of selfishness or habit – won't be alert enough to ask these questions. So help them learn to value you. Practice jumping into the conversation with your life happenings and dreams.

If they still don't honor you by listening, tell them with honesty, but kindness, that you love them but need a relationship based on equality. Let the truth be known. Live the principle of honoring. This will benefit them as much as you.

Be alert to the importance of honoring in your life. Neither domination nor subordination liberates Magnificence.

Are you ready to take a fresh look at your relationships?

What's Your Honor Rating?

List the top 10 people you spend the most time with in your life. How cherished, honored, esteemed, and empowered do you feel by each person?

		Not at all								Completely
1.	_____	1 2 3 4 5 6 7 8 9 10
2.	_____	1 2 3 4 5 6 7 8 9 10
3.	_____	1 2 3 4 5 6 7 8 9 10
4.	_____	1 2 3 4 5 6 7 8 9 10
5.	_____	1 2 3 4 5 6 7 8 9 10
6.	_____	1 2 3 4 5 6 7 8 9 10
7.	_____	1 2 3 4 5 6 7 8 9 10
8.	_____	1 2 3 4 5 6 7 8 9 10
9.	_____	1 2 3 4 5 6 7 8 9 10
10.	_____	1 2 3 4 5 6 7 8 9 10

Total score: _____ divided by 10 = _____

Your Honor Rating

1-2　Little honoring. Your Magnificence cannot come forth with so little honoring. Let yourself move into Love's embrace.

3-4　Partial honoring. You deserve more than a taste. You deserve a river of praise and honoring. This is your spiritual right.

5-6　Mediocre honoring. Imagine doubling what you are experiencing!

7-8　Substantial honoring. A lot to be grateful for – but you deserve *Magnificent* honoring!

9-10　Magnificent honoring! Now it's your turn to ensure that *everyone* around you is honored.

Magnificence Affirmation

I deserve
to be honored

*As the very creation
of infinite Love,
I am treasured
by Love*

*As Love's
beautiful expression,
I deserve to be
cherished, honored, esteemed, &
empowered*

*Being honored
is my
divine right*

*And
honoring all others
is also
my spiritual right*

Loving Yourself with Magnificence!

Here is statement #7 again from the *Liberating Your Magnificence Quiz* in the appendix.

**I surround myself with people who
cherish, honor, esteem,
& empower me.**

What are the three most powerful things you can do to align your life with this statement?

1. _____

_____

_____

2. _____

_____

_____

3. _____

_____

_____

*It is your
spiritual right
to be
surrounded by people
who honor you*

Magnificence Journal

What are you discovering in your private heart about surrounding yourself with honoring people?

_____

_____

_____

_____

_____

_____

_____

_____

_____

_____

_____

_____

_____

_____

Chapter 8

Welcome Expansion

Magnificence is expansive.

Even to say the word *Magnificence* causes one to think BIG – to think of infinity!

Yet how we resist expansion. With all the upheavals of life, we often resist expansion just to hold on to the familiar.

Think of the first time, as a little child, you held on tightly to the side of the swimming pool – afraid to let go. When many of us did let go – for a second – fear returned us instantly to the familiar edge.

Yet we learned to swim by letting go and taking the next step forward in expansion.

Today, as adults, we can use this example to move to a higher consciousness of expansion. As opportunities to expand unfold in our lives, we can learn to trust – in advance. Rather than clutching the familiar, we can welcome new opportunities and test new waters with joy and an expectation of valuable learning.

Expansion is an adventure.

***The most powerful expansions
in our lives
are often unplanned***

Think of the three most expansive things that have happened to you in your life?

1. _____

2. _____

3. _____

Did you plan them?

Here are several examples from Scott's life – in his own words – of unplanned expansions that resulted in enormous liberation:

————

I remember sitting in the newsroom where I worked as a reporter, opening my mail one day – and there it was, a draft notice to join the Army. I was surprised and unprepared mentally. This was not an expansion I had planned or welcomed!

That change, however, resulted in my first exposure to living in a third-world country (South Korea), to the beautiful children I cherished in a mountain-side orphanage, and to a worldview that was larger and more informed.

Years later, after serving for many years in an organization I admire, my department was dissolved. I had internally assumed I would be with this organization for years, if not a lifetime. This change was also unplanned and felt to me like contraction, not expansion.

Yet that very event took me to California where I eventually met and married Shannon, my best friend, soulmate, and spiritual partner, and began my career as an author – writing from the center of my life passion.

**Expansion forces us
to rise closer to our substance**

Expansion also presents itself at unexpected times. Right in the middle of writing this chapter, Scott came across a question in a book:

*"What would you do
with your life
if you knew
you could not
fail?"*

Talk about expansion!

The freedom of this question unleashed a wave of new ideas. We began envisioning a non-profit organization called *TheLoveCenter* that would train millions of individuals, couples, parents, children, teachers, and business people how to become experts in loving – to become LoveMasters. We decided that this would be our next book together. A day later, we reserved the internet name *TheLoveCenter.com* where you can find us right now.

How's that for expansive thinking?

*The closer we come
to the substance of our Life Message,
the more new opportunities
– new forms –
appear*

And the expansion continued.

Within weeks, a powerful experience of expansion took place – totally unplanned – which resulted in Shannon becoming co-author of this book.

We attended a life-transforming seminar that helped participants focus on their dreams and bring them closer to reality – and Shannon had a huge vision:

She realized that in order for her to fulfill her highest dreams – to reach all mankind with divine Love – she needed to expand her own view of her already successful healing practice.

Rather than limiting herself to serving a few hundred clients each year, she realized that she could dramatically expand her healing contribution to the world by co-authoring this book – and still maintain her healing practice with clients.

How's that for surprise expansion!

When we open ourselves to infinite expansion all that we need comes into place

Remember, the liberation of your Magnificence is inevitable! So open your heart. Resistance is futile!

In fact, think of the difference between welcoming expansion versus resisting expansion.

Welcoming expansion includes an attitude of joy, happy anticipation, eager preparation, peace, and willingness to rise to the next level.

Resisting expansion, on the other hand, includes an attitude of fear, distrust, doubt, and refusal to entertain new ideas.

- Which list sounds like Magnificence to you?
- Which attitude would most cherish and bring forward your Magnificence?

Here is an example of welcoming expansion in Shannon's life – in her own words:

When Scott and I married, I moved from Los Angeles – a city I dearly loved – to beautiful San Diego. Though I liked my new town, it felt like I was geographically at the end of the universe. I wondered what would happen to my thriving Los Angeles healing practice:

- Would my clients follow me South?
- Would I meet as many new clients in San Diego?

I recall many times sitting in my new San Diego office thinking:

"I'm alone down here. Los Angeles was such a hub of activity for me. I miss its vitality. I am concerned that I am distanced from all the liveliness that would enable my healing practice to expand."

Yet right then I challenged this closed-in feeling and reminded myself of my innate oneness with all mankind. I could never be separated from divine allness! I knew that moving back to Los Angeles was not the answer. Scott and I had been led to San Diego by Love. We both knew it.

So, sitting in my office, I affirmed that:

- I was not stuck and was, in fact, at one with all the Universe.
- My true location was not geographical, but mental. I refused to think of myself as local. I thought of my divine oneness with the entire universe.
- It is thought, not geography, which provides expansion.

When thought is encouraged
to enlarge & unfold
to greater Magnificence,
it rises to fulfillment

The results of my affirmations were healing:

- My feeling of isolation began to leave.
- I began writing metaphysical articles – and they were published. People who read my articles started calling me from New York, Florida, Arizona, Washington, and many other new places.
- Some of my articles were translated into French, Norwegian, and Portuguese.
- I became a national lecturer.
- I became co-author & speaker with Scott.

A consciousness of expansion opens us to our Magnificence

Here are four ways you can welcome expansion in your life:

1. Adopt an attitude of openness for expansion. Make space in your consciousness for the expansion and unfoldment of new ideas. Welcome new ideas.

2. Remind yourself that you are in the care of divine Love and expect your Magnificence to expand as a natural expression of *infinite* Love.

3. Listen quietly for the next unfoldment. Give yourself generous quiet time to let your Magnificence expand in thought.

4. Think of yourself as *already* including the consciousness which includes infinite expansion. Be a joyful observer of your magnificent, creative expansion.

Magnificence Affirmation

Infinite
Expansion

*In unity
with infinite Mind,
I welcome
Mind's infinitude of ideas
into my life*

*As
Mind's own expression,
I affirm that I am already equipped
to understand & utilize
each new idea
of Mind*

*I welcome Mind's
continuously expanding ideas
as new friends
in the
liberation of my Magnificence*

Loving Yourself with Magnificence!

Here is statement #8 again from the *Liberating Your Magnificence Quiz* in the appendix.

I welcome expansion
in my life.

What are the three most powerful things you can do to align your life with this statement?

1. _____

   _____

   _____

2. _____

   _____

   _____

3. _____

   _____

   _____

*It is your
spiritual right
to experience expansion
as liberating*

Magnificence Journal

How is your heart opening to expansion?

_____

_____

_____

_____

_____

_____

_____

_____

_____

_____

_____

_____

_____

_____

Chapter 9

Live
in the
Present Moment

*The
liberation
of your Magnificence
is taking place
right now*

—

not yesterday

—

not tomorrow

—

Now!

Be here *NOW!*

It is so tempting to look toward tomorrow for completion, happiness, fulfillment, and life.

For example, the two of us couldn't possibly ask for more love in our marriage. Every moment with each other is infinite fulfillment.

Yet once in a while we catch ourselves imagining the whole universe reading this book and thinking how happy we would be THEN!

That's how easy it is to be pulled out of the PRESENT moment of Magnificence – out of *NOW*.

Be here *NOW!*

When we move to *NOW*, we are forced to drop the *past* – all past shame, guilt, and regret. We are also forced to drop the *future* – all anticipation, fear, doubt, and inadequacy.

To drop the past and future in one mental breath places us in the freedom of *NOW*.

Let us find our way from the consciousness of *WHEN* to the consciousness of *NOW*.

Briefly answer this question:

I will be happy *WHEN*:

1. _____
2. _____
3. _____
4. _____
5. _____

Talk about a time trap!

The consciousness of *WHEN* is like a black hole sucking your Magnificence into oblivion – screaming in your ears, "Your Magnificence is *not NOW!*"

The consciousness of *WHEN* does not liberate Magnificence.

**The
consciousness
of NOW
is always more liberating
than the consciousness
of WHEN**

Rather than dwelling in *WHEN*, the advanced consciousness of *NOW* arrives with spiritual authority and affirms:

I am happy *NOW* because:

1. _____

2. _____

3. _____

4. _____

5. _____

The
consciousness of
NOW
moves us
into
present eternity

Be here *NOW!*
Fine, but how do I get to *NOW?*

You
arrive in
NOW
through sacred reverence
for what is
before you & within you
as
present
Magnificence

Here's what happened when Scott decided to take a break from contributing to this chapter and enter the consciousness of *NOW*.

Here are his words:

"Right *NOW*, I am happy, productive, healthy, in touch with my Life Message, sitting in the warm sun, emotionally and physically safe, in love with Shannon, completing a valuable book that is uplifting my life, and relaxed because I have taken a moment to sacredly experience *NOW*.

I am surrounded by quietness and tinkling bells in the wind next door – and the soft cooing of a morning dove. I wasn't even aware of these beautiful sounds just moments ago. They did not exist in my consciousness outside of *NOW*.

The peace that is descending within me in this sacred silence is opening me to inner calm. My dream with Shannon to bring all mankind into the heart of Love returns to inner consciousness as I mentally embrace the world's needs. I silently share my peace with all mankind.

I resist the habit to return to planning or speculating. I feel refreshed by *NOW*. I feel in touch with abundance. Here, *NOW*, my needs are met. I am without fear or doubt. I feel centered in Love – my being, my *substance*.

I see with insight how *form* is so related to time. When I leave this consciousness of *NOW*, I will adopt some *form* – husband, writer, speaker, driver.

I feel more aware of a desire to carry this *NOW* consciousness forward –– to move, not through time events, but in a flow of *NOW* consciousness that radiates my pure *substance* even when the events of my life are labeled time, space, activities, or tasks.

I see that the only real event is consciousness unfolding. I feel empowered by my inner centeredness. What started as a short trip to *NOW* has moved me to eternity consciousness.

The consciousness of NOW connects us to eternal Truth

Now it's your turn.

Look around you with sacred reverence and sink into *NOW*. Let go of your entire past. Just let it go. And let go of all that you anticipate or hope for tomorrow. Let it go. Sink into *NOW*. Allow yourself to value:

What is present – *Now!*

What you see – *Now!*

What you feel – *Now!*

What is Magnificent – *Now!*

To enter NOW is to see, feel, & acknowledge Love's Presence

NOW is contagious. Only a few tastes makes you hungry for more.

NOW is a divine moment – a moment of pure Magnificence outside of all time.

We can never experience Magnificence outside of *NOW*. Yet how often do we flow through an entire

day without one moment of *NOW?*   Isn't that
ridiculous?

Magnificence
only occurs
in
NOW

So how do we hold on to *NOW* consciousness?

By leaving the consciousness of *time.*

Think of *time* as a thought-prison holding you
captive in the past or future.

If, for example, you put off Magnificence until a
better moment, you've been snookered.   You're in
time prison. And if you constantly review your past,
you are still in time prison. The only way to escape is
to relinquish time itself.

Here's one great approach.

Take your next steps in life – whatever you are
doing – in *Slow Motion Enjoy Mode*:

- If you are walking, slow down to a
  ridiculously slow speed and *feel* your
  steps. What do you observe *NOW?*   A
  blade of grass or single flower in *Slow
  Motion Enjoy Mode* comes passionately
  into existence and beauty.

- The next time you see your spouse, your
  kids, or a good friend, hug them in *Slow
  Motion Enjoy Mode.* Let the hug continue
  and continue and continue as each of
  you enjoys eternal L   O   V   E.

- When you are driving home and about a
  half block from your house, slow your car
  to 2 mph. As you creep slowly towards
  your home, what do you see that you
  never saw before?

- Turn the next page of this book with extraordinary slowness. Notice how the page *feels* in your fingers. Then note the off-white color and the amount of open space on the page.

Be here *NOW!*

Every
taste of NOW
unites us to eternity
&
opens us
to Magnificence

Magnificence Affirmation
Now

*I am able
to move outside
of all time
to
Now*

*I am able
to feel, see, embrace, & enjoy
the full Magnificence
that is
present NOW*

*I am able
to be
at one with
Now*

Loving Yourself with Magnificence!

Here is statement #9 again from the *Liberating Your Magnificence Quiz* in the appendix.

**I live fully in the present moment,
not in the past or future.**

What are the three most powerful things you can do to align your life with this statement?

1. _____

_____

_____

2. _____

_____

_____

3. _____

_____

_____

*It is your
spiritual right
to experience
NOW!*

Magnificence Journal

What are you discovering about *NOW* and your Magnificence?

_____

_____

_____

_____

_____

_____

_____

_____

_____

_____

_____

_____

_____

Chapter 10

Trust the Power of Love

Love is the greatest force in the universe.

One day, while we were at Disneyland, Scott noticed a little girl crying uncontrollably in the midst of a sea of passing people.

Scott kneeled down to her.

"What's wrong sweetie?" he asked.

"My mommy is gone," she blurted through tears.

"I will stay with you until we find your Mom," Scott said. At that moment, Scott made the decision to trust Love to bring about the correct solution.

Instantly, she stopped crying. The force of Love was already at work healing her heart – assuring her of good to come.

Her Mom soon found us.

That was all.

But it made us think.

This little girl was crying for her Mom, but Love surprised her with an unexpected solution – Scott.

- Can we – as adults – trust Love for solutions to our life problems with the same openness as the little girl?
- Can you let this book take your hand and lead you home to your Magnificence?
- Are you prepared for the surprise of Love?

Trust Love.

Those words seem too simple.

Can Love really be that significant a force in the liberation of our Magnificence?

When Scott's Dad was a young father, he was diagnosed with a brain tumor. The doctors had no remedy and gave him only a few months to live.

Such a moment forces one to make big choices.

His Dad decided to trust Love and was led to put his trust in spiritual healing. It was more than blind faith. It was a deep spiritual receptivity which led to a new understanding of his spiritual perfection – that his health was anchored in spirituality.

And he was healed! The same doctors, a year later, could find no trace of the tumor. He lived a full life – and many decades more. For Scott, this meant an entire lifetime of growing up with his Dad and the example of universal, healing love he imparted to Scott.

Love upheld his Dad's Magnificence.

This also taught his entire family the power of trusting Love for guidance. And it led to a lifetime of spiritual healings.

Trust Love.

In the quiet sanctuary of our individual prayers, Love comes to us. It may not come as the same answer for each of us. Love often surprises.

There is no
greater power
than divine Love
for the
total liberation
of your Magnificence

When Shannon's former marriage ended, after 18 years, she was devastated. A year later, when we first met, it was hard for her to trust the possibility of a successful relationship with another man.

But Love surprised her!

Love came to her in the form of a man (Scott) who lived and breathed unconditional love. Love honored her Magnificence and lifted her into liberation. Today, we write and speak together as "The Love Team."

Trust Love.

Shannon also deeply trusted Love in raising her daughter Kai. Here are her words:

When I first became a mother, the love in me was almost unimaginable! I felt motherhood to be my holiest charge. But with that love came an overwhelming sense of responsibility for my daughter's care:

- How can I raise her and teach her sufficiently so she will grow up happy?
- What can I tell her so she'll be safe and make wise decisions?
- Is there a way to teach her without lecturing my values to her?

I prayed about this for a long time – and the answer came in a surprising way to me.

I remember the moment my prayers were answered. I was standing in front of the refrigerator with the door wide open, looking for something to prepare for dinner. Divine guidance doesn't always choose the most convenient time to unfold!

At that exact moment, I received instruction from divine Love to teach Kai to turn to angel thoughts –

to divine Mind – for direction and to teach her to do this for herself. Kai was about 3 years old.

"What a great idea!" I thought. "I'll do that!"

Meanwhile Kai was at my knee, hanging on, and feeling a little tired and bored. She rarely nagged, but this day was as close as she came to it.

Kai persisted to tug at my thought for attention as I stood there thinking about dinner – but just then the angel thought unfolded again: "Teach her to lean on angel thoughts! Do it now!"

I felt it was a divine direction. This time I didn't hesitate to respond. I leaned down and spoke to her lovingly:

"Kai, I think we need divine guidance. We need divine Love's angel thoughts to tell us what to do right now."

She stared at me, listening, still a little whiny.

I continued:

"Will you listen to angel thoughts with me and see what we are being guided to do?"

I could tell she was trying to understand what I was telling her. She'd heard about angel thoughts before, but it hadn't registered.

"Will you listen with Mommy to hear angel thoughts?" I asked. She agreed.

I turned back to face the decision about dinner and the angel thought said: "Don't leave her alone to listen to angel thoughts. Pray with her."

Yikes! It would have been a set up for failure to leave her unsupported and alone. I had prayed about this very subject as a top priority since I was pregnant and suddenly, when I now had the answer to my prayer, I was more concerned with making the dinner menu the top priority!

Right then I became a prayer supporter for Kai. I quit thinking about dinner and silently reminded myself: "We include all Love's angel thoughts of divine guidance this very moment, and we know it."

I quietly listened to Love.

The next time I thought of it again, I was putting broccoli in the steamer and I thought, "Where is Kai? I haven't seen her for the last 10 minutes." That in itself was unusual for me. Yet I felt peaceful as I questioned her location.

Love led me down the hall where she was in her room, happily putting Snoopy to bed ever so sweetly.

I thought, "Divine Love, thank you!"

Then I decided to make sure Kai had made the connection too.

"Kai! Look at you! Do you know that since we asked Love's angel thoughts to guide us, that they led you to your room and gave you the wonderful idea to put Snoopy to bed? Look at how harmonious you are! Isn't this happy? Aren't we glad we asked the angel thoughts for help when we were in the kitchen?"

I spoke another sentence or two when I saw her eyes tell me she got it. She made the connection.

Thank you, God!

I knew then that this would always be our place of reference for all our problems, from the tiniest to the grandest.

I knew that as we went through the years together, our relationship would be one where we would be led to ask for angel thoughts about absolutely everything.

And so it was. Kai learned early that she had a prayer partner in me. Just as I have a total dependence on divine guidance each day, from the time I rise to the time I go to bed, she learned from a tender age the great comfort in trusting Love to guide her.

Trust Love.

This is the advice I would give any parent.

Listen to angel thoughts to guide you. They lead to all blessings, especially the ones you can access in no other way.

Trust
Love's angel thoughts
to guide you and keep you
in the Light

Trust Love.

Shift trust from unproductive, restricting mental habits such as:

- Trusting in luck – to win the lottery or be protected on the freeway.
- Trusting in time to make things better.
- Trusting in another person rather than in divine Love.

Such trusts are neither powerful nor liberating.

Think of replacing these trusts with whole-hearted leaning on the pillar of infinite Love at all times and for all decisions.

Trusting Love is not passive.

If we trust Love as the Principle of the universe, that means we can reliably trust the directions of Love.

These directions come to us in our intuition as we unite with Love's consciousness.

Trust Love.

These words can be applied in the simplest of ways to guide you to Magnificence.

For example, what are the three most important things on your to-do list for today? You will learn a big lesson if you actually write them here:

1. _____

2. _____

3. _____

Now, ask yourself *Love's Question*:

What are the three most important things you are led *by Love* to do today?

1. _____

2. _____

3. _____

How's that for revealing?

Imagine going through the rest of your life from the consciousness of the first to-do list rather than living your life from the consciousness of Love's list.

Asking
Love's Question
lifts us to the consciousness that
liberates Magnificence

Magnificence Affirmation

Trust Love

*As I listen
to my deepest intuition,
I hear
Love's message*

*Love
is filling
my consciousness
with
angel thoughts*

*I trust
& release
my entire life
to
Love's Magnificence*

Loving Yourself with Magnificence!

Here is statement #10 again from the *Liberating Your Magnificence Quiz* in the appendix.

**I trust the power of Love
to liberate my Magnificence.**

What are the three most powerful things you can do to align your life with this statement?

1. _____

   _____

   _____

2. _____

   _____

   _____

3. _____

   _____

   _____

*It is your
spiritual right
to trust
Love*

Magnificence Journal

Where is divine Love leading you right now in the liberation of your Magnificence?

_____

_____

_____

_____

_____

_____

_____

_____

_____

_____

_____

_____

_____

_____

Chapter 11

Become
an Expert at
Spiritual Affirmations

We are all moving into Light.

We are advancing together in a spiritual Millennium that is lifting our consciousness to Truth. Spirituality has become the *substance* of the advanced message.

> **The
> moment has arrived for
> all of us
> to become experts
> in understanding and utilizing
> the power
> of
> spirituality**

You are holding in your hands a book that is speaking to you directly from Truth. It could not be otherwise since the liberation of your Magnificence is a *spiritual* event.

Hence this powerful, glorious *fact* – your liberation is inevitable!

Peek ahead at the chapters to come. We will be facing and dissolving all the beliefs of limitation – doubt, guilt, lack, fear, anger, time, age, rejection, and overwhelm – that would prevent your Magnificence from pouring forth.

To live in the heart of our Magnificence, we need to rise together into expertise as spiritual thinkers.

For example, think of the thousands of thoughts that present themselves to you each day. The thoughts you accept, hold close, and rehearse represent continual affirmations – either positive or negative.

How many times, for example, have you repeatedly and silently affirmed to yourself?

- I'm tired.
- I'm lonely.
- I'm aging.
- I'm worried.
- I need more money.
- I don't feel loved.
- I feel weak or ill.
- I feel limited and trapped.

Such negative affirmations, poured repeatedly into consciousness, do not support the expression of Magnificence. That's why we all need to became *masters* of spiritual affirmations.

Spiritual affirmations,
finely tuned
to Truth,
dissolve limitations
&
transform consciousness
into Light

We have entered a Millennium of sacred unity where civilization is advancing to a greater understanding of spiritual identity.

We have all gathered together for a universal spiritual launch, even though the individual paths that have led us to this shared moment are diverse.

So let us affirm:

> *We are not being called*
> *to judge each other,*
> *but to*
> *come together*
> *– in unity –*
> *to a spiritual awareness*
> *that will liberate*
> *universal*
> *Magnificence*

In that spirit of unity and universal Love, let us explore six principles of effective spiritual affirmations that give us the power to heal.

Six Principles
of Effective
Spiritual Affirmations

Principle 1:   Effective affirmations acknowledge a **Higher Power** – God, divine Love, or whatever name resonates with your highest spiritual understanding.

Principle 2:   Effective affirmations acknowledge our **oneness** with this Higher Power – our oneness with infinite Love.

Principle 3:   Effective affirmations acknowledge that **we are the creation & expression** of this Higher Power.

Principle 4:   Effective affirmations acknowledge that **our true substance is spiritual**.

Principle 5:   Effective affirmations acknowledge that **our motive & desire is to be in harmony with divine law,** not to manipulate divine law for individual gain.

Principle 6:   Effective affirmations acknowledge that all-inclusive **Love is present, available, & evident now** – for all mankind.

Here is a profound truth underlying our inherent ability to heal:

***We are
not material beings
trying to use spiritual affirmations
to solve finite problems***

***We are
spiritual beings
who already include and express
infinite, divine solutions***

Effective affirmations are preceded by an awareness of our sacred identity – our divine origin.

The biggest belief we suffer from is that we could be separate from Love. All pain, suffering, and fear occurs from this belief that we are – or could be – divisible, detached, or severed from Love.

Feelings that we have been rejected, condemned, or abandoned attempt to confirm the illusion that we are separate from Love.

The true purpose of making affirmations is to remind us of our oneness with Love and align our consciousness with divine Truth.

***Our affirmations
have the power
to conquer, liberate, and heal
only
when they come from
divine Love –
the Source of our being***

When we experience our oneness with divine Love, we can think boldly from this power and affirm:

- I am the true Magnificence of divine Love!
- Everyone I see or hold in my conscious-ness is the true Magnificence of divine Love!
- Together we are one with all Love and its radiance of Magnificence, expressed as the divine us!

And we can do this in the simplest of ways and in the most ordinary of circumstances.

Take the example of being stuck in freeway traffic. Even in such a mundane situation, you can view this as a mental opportunity to practice affirmations.

Challenge the thought which is pulling and tugging at your spirituality and peace. It is only your *thought* that suggests you are in a state of frustration and stress.

You can either accept thoughts which would label you as a victim, or acknowledge the true picture of Love's ever-presence in your life – even in a traffic jam. In other words, choose to leave the paradigm of limitation. You can, for example, affirm:

- I see myself, not stuck in traffic, but open right now to infinity – to progress, creativity, expansion, mobility, wisdom, inspiration, power, peacefulness, and all good.
- I see myself fully empowered right now with freedom to acknowledge my true identity and oneness with Love.
- I see myself empowered to look around me and see the infinite expression of Love everywhere I look – in every car and within every person around me.

Such thinking moves you instantly into a consciousness of infinite possibility and Love. This is the consciousness that both heals and liberates Magnificence!

The liberating choice is always yours:

- You can choose your thoughts wisely throughout the day.
- You can detach yourself from thoughts which rehearse negativity.
- You can choose to experience life outside the paradigm of circumstances or limitation.
- You can choose to observe reality with unlimited possibilities of good.

When you
think and live
from the consciousness
of your oneness with Love,
your reality
will manifest
Love

Affirmation Practice

Let's practice utilizing the full power of spiritual affirmations. Which of the following affirmations would most advance your Magnificence?

Affirmation A

I am working at
becoming a loving person
and expressing love to the world

Affirmation B

I am,
at this exact moment,
the Magnificent expression
of Love.
I am filled with Love
that radiates compassion & healing power
to all the world

Affirmation A comes from a loving heart, but affirmation B draws us higher into spiritual power.

There is an immense difference between thinking of yourself as *working at* becoming a loving person versus knowing yourself *as* the very radiance of infinite Love.

Thinking that we are trying, seeking, getting better, working at, or slowly improving defines us as separated from the Higher Power and not at one with this power.

The truth that underlies our Magnificence is that we are never separate from Love, Spirit, Truth, Light.

In Truth, we are the outcome – the expression, the radiance – of spiritual Light.

We can practice and strengthen our affirmations from this mental position of oneness.

Oneness
with Spirit
is our inherent identity
and is the
Source
of our Magnificence

Here is another pair of affirmations. Which one
has the greatest spiritual strength?

Affirmation A

I affirm
that I am
at one
with divine Light
and I will therefore
get the job I have applied for today
and at the salary I want

Affirmation B

I affirm
that I am at one
with divine Mind
and that I therefore, right now,
include
all the ideas & opportunities within Mind –
my perfect place in the universe,
my perfect activity, abundant supply,
and
a perpetual state of Love's fulfillment.
I also affirm
that this is true for
all mankind

Affirmation A acknowledges oneness with
divinity, but limits itself by putting the emphasis on
a predetermined *form* – a specific job and salary
desired.

Affirmation B rises higher because it trusts
divine Light – the *ideas* of Mind and the *fulfillment* of

Love – to unfold the highest *forms* in our life, even beyond what we might have desired.

This is true abundance!

> *If we are*
> *wise enough to know that*
> *the Higher Power*
> *is spiritual,*
> *we must also*
> *be wise enough to know that*
> *the outcome of our affirmations*
> *must also be spiritual*

When we raise our affirmations to their highest power, we are often surprised with totally different – and better – results than those we had outlined ourselves.

Affirmation B also has great power because it acknowledges that abundance embraces all mankind – acknowledging our universal oneness with Love.

As you move through the rest of this book and address all the *beliefs* and *claims* that would attempt to block your liberation, keep moving to the highest spiritual ground in your affirmations.

Test your affirmations against the six spiritual principles. Enjoy rising into the power and presence of Spirit.

> *It is your*
> *spiritual right*
> *to think, speak, & live*
> *with the*
> *complete authority*
> *of Spirit*

Denials & Affirmations

Here is a powerful way to move thought to high spiritual ground – an approach used almost every morning by Shannon.

Here are her words:

Often, when I begin my morning prayers, I ground myself in the fact that I am turning to divine Love for all inspiration and guidance. Then I take a yellow pad and briefly jot down all the negative claims which need to be challenged in my life. I put them in a column on the left. And I keep them brief.

Then I boldly state the affirmation – the spiritual Truth – that knocks out and replaces each negative claim. I make sure the affirmations are generous and sufficient to outweigh the negative thoughts. I am listening to Love for these affirmations.

One morning, for example, my list of negative thoughts included fear, fatigue, stress, congestion, and concern over money. I also felt I needed to heal fears regarding the health and protection of a family member who lives hundreds of miles away.

I then dissolved these intrusive thoughts attempting to rob me of my spiritual freedom and dominion.

Here is what I affirmed:

- I am the expression of Love and I therefore live in divine assurance (my spiritual response to fear).
- I am resting in Mind and I am continually refreshed with new energies and strength (my spiritual response to fatigue).

- I live in divine peace and I experience continual harmony, exempt from beliefs of time & space & limitation (my spiritual response to stress).
- I am open to all good with all my channels filled with free-flowing Love (my spiritual response to congestion).
- I am aware of the infinite abundance of good manifesting itself continually as mine (my spiritual response to limited money).
- I see my family member expressing Love's complete care, protection, and healing – and therefore safe, secure, healthy, and whole (my spiritual response to family protection).
- I know all these affirmations to be true.
- I experience them in full force, right now at this moment in eternity, because I am at one with infinite Love.

Allowing each of these truths to reveal themselves so clearly in my consciousness presented a true picture of reality and brought immediate healing.

Bold
affirmations
of Truth & Love
liberate our Magnificence

Your Turn

Briefly list the negative thoughts seeking legitimacy in your life right now:

Now replace these thoughts with the most powerful spiritual affirmations that come to you as the expression of omnipotent Truth and Love:

Asking for Guidance

Always remember how simply you can find answers from divine Love.

**Be
like a child
and ask divine Love
for guidance – in everything**

There is nothing too small or unimportant to ask for Love's guidance.

- What should I wear?
- What should I be thinking about that person or event?
- What response should I give to...?
- How am I doing?
- What step should I take next for true progress?

Think of guidance as a three step package:

1. Ask for guidance.
2. Remember to listen for it.
3. Always give thanks.

It is simple – like all things of Spirit.

Practicing these three steps will cause you to realize, expand, and enjoy your sacred relationship with Love. Such prayers are always answered.

**Listening continually for
Love's guidance
is living in oneness
with
divine Love**

Magnificence Affirmation
Affirmation Power

*I am able
to make
bold, powerful, & effective
spiritual affirmations
because I am
the very expression
of divine Love*

*I am able
to think & act
with healing power
because Spirit
– divine Love, Truth, Light –
is expressing me
as It's
Magnificence*

*I affirm
that all mankind is included in my
healing affirmations
of Truth*

Loving Yourself with Magnificence!

Here is statement #11 again from the *Liberating Your Magnificence Quiz* in the appendix.

I am an expert
at making spiritual affirmations

What are the three most powerful things you can do to align your life with this statement?

1. _____

   _____

   _____

2. _____

   _____

   _____

3. _____

   _____

   _____

It is your
spiritual right
to make
bold and effective
spiritual affirmations

Magnificence Journal

What is the most empowering thing you have learned about making spiritual affirmations?

_____

_____

_____

_____

_____

_____

_____

_____

_____

_____

_____

_____

_____

_____

_____

Stage 3

Free
Your
Magnificence

Chapter 12

Dump Doubt
For a Life
of Soul

As you take bold steps to claim and live your Magnificence, what else would you expect to immediately appear – monster-size – than the dragon of doubt!

Can you imagine any other enemy with more ability to push you off the path of your dreams?

It is of immense value to see doubt, not as a personal battle with self-esteem, but as a collective challenge – in world consciousness – to the liberation of Magnificence.

When we look at doubt in this objective, rather than personal way, our mentality begins to laugh at doubt – to see it for the *illusion* it is.

Note the word *illusion.* Even if an illusion seems to have enormous, monstrous, dragon-like power, it is nevertheless an illusion. No reality! No existence! No power!

Think of the people throughout the world who are right now reading this chapter along with you. What percent of them do you think are feeling the oppressive weight of self-doubt? Far too many.

Here is the solution. By recognizing that doubt is not a personal issue, but a challenge to *collective* consciousness, we rise to the defense, not just of our Magnificence, but to the defense of all mankind's Magnificence.

This is the liberation consciousness that denounces and demotes doubt to the dust.

It is our spiritual right to live in the freedom of Soul rather than in the dungeon of doubt

Freedom of Soul.

Don't those words just breeze through your inner being like a refreshing drink of opportunity? That is the mental perspective that lifts us into freedom.

Rather than spending our energy attempting to defeat doubt, let us utilize the very same energy to live out from the freedom of Soul.

The two of us have learned to do this in our own lives – with great liberation. Here is an example in Scott's own words:

One example of moving from doubt to Soul occurred when I was elected to conduct services at a local church. You would think that this, by it's very nature, would have made expressing Soul a piece of cake. But it is very easy to fall into the dungeon of doubt and think:

- Will I be as good as the previous person?
- Will I please them?
- Am I qualified?

Well, I decided, forget that! I live in Soul and I'm going to let Soul express me in its infinite boldness and divine grace.

And so I did. I internally let Soul lift me to Soul's own expression of universal love and power. I quit thinking about anyone's reaction. My real job, I reasoned, was to express Soul. Or, more accurately, to let Soul express me – with Magnificence and without reservation.

Wow!

Can you imagine what this did to my whole life?

My life became full of radiance, joy, freedom, and boundless expression. The inner admission of my right to freedom led to joy in conducting the church services, creative self expression in my entire life, and the writing of *The Love You Deserve*.

Get a taste of living out from Soul and you'll never return to doubt

Here is Shannon's story of overcoming doubt as a mother.

When my daughter was a toddler, I had a severe attack of self-doubt. I was a stay-at-home Mom – something that I relished. But after several years of being out of the job market, I was torn between staying full time in my mothering role or doing part-time work.

As I went through the process of seeing what I could qualify for on a part-time basis, I couldn't even justify the cost of child care, much less feel I was doing anything meaningful.

It was a moment of great self-doubt:

- Did I have any value to the world?
- Was my daughter the only person in the universe in need of me?
- What would I do when she began school?

The future looked bleak with opportunity for me. I felt on the verge of tears on many days.

While this "stuck" mode continued for a few months, I persevered with prayer. In my prayers, I reminded myself that my eternal life had meaning, relevance, and value to the universe. I prayed to be useful.

It was at this time that I met a lovely, new girlfriend. Her name was Mona, and she was desperate for help in her business. I became her assistant and worked part-time to relieve her in her growing school of art.

As Mona and I worked together and became close, I learned of her deep desire to write a book so that everyone could learn to draw.

It was my privilege to act on her support team to bring that about. Her book and art teaching method – known now as Monart School of the Arts – have transformed lives and her book has been translated into many languages.

Mona expressed greatness and I was by her side while her Magnificence was being ushered in. For me, it was a rich opportunity to express my love for the earth's children.

We both realized our Magnificence.

Love
is right now calling forth
your Magnificence
&
enabling you to release
all doubt for
the freedom of Soul

Magnificence Affirmation

The freedom
of Soul

Doubt
has no reality
in the infinite power and freedom
of Soul

Because I am
Love's creation & expression,
I am able
to open my entire life
to Soul's Light
& live
in the complete freedom of Soul

Soul
is calling forth
all mankind
to live in
divine assurance

Loving Yourself with Magnificence!

Here is statement #12 again from the *Liberating Your Magnificence Quiz* in the appendix.

**I live in the freedom of Soul
rather than in the dungeon of doubt.**

What are the three most powerful things you can do to align your life with this statement?

1. _____
   _____
   _____

2. _____
   _____
   _____

3. _____
   _____
   _____

*It is your
spiritual right
to live in the
freedom
of
Soul*

Magnificence Journal

What is Soul calling you forth to know and be as the fullest expression of your Magnificence?

_____

_____

_____

_____

_____

_____

_____

_____

_____

_____

_____

_____

_____

_____

Chapter 13

Rise
from Guilt
Into
Spiritual Freedom

"I don't do guilt!"

That about sums up Shannon's posture on the subject.

Scott, on the other hand, used to be quite proficient at guilt – past, present, or even future. When Shannon arrived, however, the mental weather dramatically changed – thankfully. Instead of guilt came the healing currents of:

- Spiritual freedom, and
- Innocence

What a giant relief!

And here's a liberation news flash:

Those words – spiritual freedom and innocence – also describe *you* and your new life of total liberation.

> *Spiritual freedom*
> *& innocence*
> *allow your*
> *Magnificence*
> *to come out from hiding*
> *and*
> *shine!*

Let's face it, guilt is a heavy load.

It's so easy to feel guilty about things left undone and things that are regrettable. Guilt is like an enormous burden that feels like a permanent attachment to our consciousness.

Being full of guilt is like waking up in the morning, immediately reaching for a backpack, loading it with 45 pounds of cement, slinging it on your back, and heading to the shower – and then carrying it continuously for the rest of the day as your own personal load of guilt.

That is not a life of liberation.

Few things in life are *less* liberating than guilt. Guilt acts as an obstacle to our going forward and it acts to imprint us with feeling undeserving.

It's time for all of us to say:

"I don't do guilt!"

Let's start right now.

Quickly identify the areas in your life where you feel any guilt. Get it out in the open. Go ahead, take a moment and make a list. We'll even give you the whole next page:

My Very Own Personal
Guilt Page

Here is the load of guilt I openly or secretly drag behind me everywhere I go in life:

You
are now authorized
by your own Magnificence
to draw a line through all this mental weight,
release it from your life,
and rise into
spiritual freedom

Everything on your personal guilt page is a mere collection of *thoughts*. These *thoughts* are the heavy burden. And you have the total power to delete them – because they are only *thoughts*.

Let Love dissolve these thoughts into pure spiritual freedom and innocence.

It is your choice.

When Shannon entered Scott's life with the spiritual freedom to say "I don't do guilt," Scott felt such a wave of unconditional love that guilt could no longer attach itself to him either. He became free.

That's how *you* deserve to feel – no matter how deeply you are suffering.

So right now, think of us supporting you. Accept us as entering your life with unconditional love and spiritual freedom to support your complete disposal of guilt.

Did you draw a line through your guilt page?

Go ahead. Do it!

We guarantee that, if we ever visit you, we are going to immediately turn to that page in your book to make sure you did!

***It is your
spiritual right
to live
the rest of your life
without guilt***

Nailing Guilt
from Within and Without

As we go forward together, claiming our spiritual freedom and innocence, let's become astute at preventing guilt from creeping into consciousness – from any source.

For example, guilt often sneaks in from the past.

Who doesn't have things they'd love to change about their behavior in the past? Dwelling in the past, however, puts us on a treadmill of *present* non-progress. We find ourselves perpetually saying, "If only...."

The cycle needs to be broken.

The
consciousness of Magnificence
refuses guilt from
the past

Here is a simple exercise to stop the past from haunting you in the present.

When you become aware of guilt from the past, immediately become your own best friend. Come to your defense – big time! Become a prosecutor to the guilt:

- Instantly argue against it's intelligence or value in your life.
- Love yourself.
- Affirm to yourself: "I don't do guilt!"
- Forgive yourself. You cannot put the toothpaste back into the tube. It's a waste of time and won't work. Let it go.
- Thank yourself that you have learned to make better decisions.

- Decide with *present* spiritual freedom and innocence that you will not repeat the mistake – nor repeat the shame.
- Give yourself the love you'd give your best friend. Let your inner light warm your own heart with renewed feelings of your goodness, value, and worth. You deserve to feel wonderful this very moment. If not now, when?
- Stay in the now. Now is always full of more than we can possibly accept of abundant good. Receive it!
- Claim your innocence. Name yourself as innocent and good. This really is your true self – pure and beautiful.
- Walk in the permanent light of your spiritual freedom and innocence. This is your inherent spiritual identity.

Another bold way to move beyond guilt is to apologize.

There have been many times when Shannon and I have apologized to each other and instantly released any blame or guilt.

The
consciousness of Magnificence
apologizes rapidly
and moves
forward

If you need to call someone right now to apologize, put down this book and do it. This is part of your liberation. If you can't call them or it would be unwise to do so, write out your apology on the next page. Even if it's not appropriate to send it, writing out this apology will be healing.

I apologize

Dear _____:

I apologize for:

**The faster
you apologize,
the faster you enter
liberation**

It is natural to wish we hadn't made mistakes, natural to wish we had done better.

Think of how you were at age 18. Yikes! And each decade after that. But who you are today is the best that you've done so far.

We all have more work to do, but thank God, we have eternity for our enlightenment! We've been learning lessons all our lives. It's time to really get this lesson on guilt and move on!

Do you want to blast forward in the liberation of your Magnificence right now?

Then become an expert at forgiveness.

The
consciousness of Magnificence
forgives rapidly

Think of those in your past who have caused you hurt or suffering. Go ahead. Forgive them – right now – for any hurt feelings they may have caused.

Now forgive yourself as you just forgave them.

Do this with each person in your past or present where guilt remains.

Forgiveness
has extraordinary power
both to
heal & liberate
your
Magnificence

Experience the new freedom.

Experience yourself replacing guilt with thoughts of love for yourself. Then let your love embrace everyone else in your entire consciousness.

***Every step
you take away from guilt
into spiritual freedom and innocence
is a step of liberation
for everyone
in your consciousness***

Refuse to accept guilt – even if it is imposed on you by others. Whether intentional or not, put up your defenses and become a spiritual warrior. Guilt is destructive to Magnificence and needs to be seen and healed instantly.

Sometimes other people may feel you should have done something differently and lay their disappointment at your feet.

But it's up to you whether you pick it up.

Don't!

Others may use guilt to manipulate you into doing something – and this can be very subtle and deceptive. In fact, the person may or may not be aware of their inflicting guilt. Either way, it must be dealt with.

Once you are aware of the guilt, confront it in your own thinking.

For example, if a family member or friend says something that carries a guilt trail, notice the way you feel. If it's guilt, detach yourself from it at once and remind yourself of your innocence – and their innocence. Move your consciousness instantly into spiritual freedom.

The solution to someone manipulating you to feel guilt, whether intended or not, is to refuse it. If you accept guilt thoughts, then you will, for sure, begin to feel the guilt as well. You will feel like you are wrong. Refuse this thought. Claim your spiritual right to govern yourself free of guilt.

Then take another step towards liberation. See the other person as separate from any aspect of guilt as well.

Perceive them as innocent of guilt-infliction. Make the separation of the error from the person. Everyone, now, is free. Seal this freedom with a recording in your journal of how it feels and why it is right to feel guiltless.

If guilt is a continual reoccurrence with certain friends, tighten your inner circle to include only those who affirm your spiritual freedom and innocence. And make sure you yourself are *always* seeing and supporting innocence and freedom in others.

People who are not spiritually aware often blame others rather than face their own demons. Love them, but let them loose from your Magnificent team.

Cut the string that ties you together and release them to find their own way. Let spiritual freedom and innocence govern your life.

You
have been called forth
by Love
to live in liberation
from guilt

Magnificence Affirmation

Spiritual Freedom
& Innocence

*I am
the expression
of divine
innocence and goodness*

*I am
the consciousness
of spiritual
freedom*

*My
innocence & spiritual freedom
are right now
liberating everyone I have known
freeing us jointly
to rise
into Magnificence*

Loving Yourself with Magnificence!

Here is statement #13 again from the *Liberating Your Magnificence Quiz* in the appendix.

I live without guilt.

What are the three most powerful things you can do to align your life with this statement?

1. _____

   _____

   _____

2. _____

   _____

   _____

3. _____

   _____

   _____

It is your
spiritual right
to live in spiritual freedom
&
innocence

Magnificence Journal

What are you learning about your spiritual freedom and innocence?

_____

_____

_____

_____

_____

_____

_____

_____

_____

_____

_____

_____

_____

_____

_____

_____

Chapter 14

Choose
the Consciousness of
Abundance

You have a Magnificent choice – right now!
You can either:

1. Live in the consciousness of poverty
    which screams and moans, "I lack."

or

2. Live in the consciousness of abundance
    which rejoices and exclaims, "I include."

It is a mental choice.

For example, one day we were driving together on a trip and took time, as we often do, to share our innermost thoughts with each other.

Scott went first: "Shannon, right now I feel burdened by the need for more money and what we are lacking." Shannon let out a huge laugh (not what Scott expected as a reply) and said: "I was just feeling how deeply grateful I am for our enormous abundance."

Well, we're married, have the same bank account, and we work closely together. How could we have such opposite answers when our *circumstances* were identical?

Abundance or lack is a state of consciousness, not a state of circumstances

Shannon was experiencing the consciousness of abundance at the simultaneous moment that Scott was drowning in the consciousness of lack.

This was a revealing moment and lesson.

An even greater lesson, however, took place almost immediately after we married each other. It was shocking, but it forced us instantly to choose between a consciousness of poverty or a consciousness of abundance.

This is really Shannon's story, so here it is in her words:

In the very first year of our marriage, I was dragged into a lawsuit that seemed overwhelming and lasted almost two years.

Within months, Scott and I went through all our savings and then some. The evidence of lack was overwhelming – lack of justice, lack of funds to fight injustice, lack of emotional energy to withstand the onslaught, and lack of hope.

I was the underdog of underdogs.

The negative thoughts that attacked my consciousness were:

- I'm out of money.
- It looks like I will go bankrupt.
- I'm the victim of someone's dishonesty, theft, and unfairness.

- I'm scared.
- I can't win.
- This could create disease in me.
- I feel desperate.
- I am so angry.
- I haven't had a good night's sleep or peace in months.

What power was within me to counter this onslaught of negative thought-attacks?

For almost twenty years, I had developed great trust and understanding in the power of spiritual healing, my chosen occupation. In my spiritual work, I had constantly seen the powerful effects of approaching life with the consciousness of abundance rather than with the consciousness of lack. This had become my daily consciousness and I knew it was going to be my biggest weapon.

And it was!

In my consistent affirmations of spiritual abundance, I mentally denounced what appeared to be overwhelming lack.

The result of taking this mental, spiritual stand and staying in the consciousness of abundance was an amazing series of events:

First, a phenomenal attorney came into my life with courage, spiritual conviction, and ability to penetrate to the hidden truth.

Second, as the case expanded, another company became involved in the lawsuit to protect their interests. They took over all my legal bills – and the final tally was close to two million dollars!

What looked like a situation of irreparable harm to me turned into infinite possibilities of good. Though I was still heavily involved in the lawsuit, I was able to release the burden of legal fees.

Third, the case was settled with my name exonerated. In fact, far more significant than resolving the case, I felt that my attorney, a man I will respect for eternity, had powerfully and effectively defended my womanhood.

It was also vital – *after* the case – to stay in the consciousness of abundance.

I had a choice.

I could look back on the ordeal as a crippling emotional and financial experience, draining Scott's and my energies both professionally and personally, not to mention being the major event of the first two years of our marriage. Although such thinking might seem reasonable, it would have landed me right back in a consciousness of lack.

I chose instead – but not without struggle and affirmations – to look back on this experience from the consciousness of abundance, not lack. Here is the abundant gain I see today as I look back:

- A phenomenal strengthening of the bond of love between Scott and me in our first years of marriage and the extraordinary evidence of the power of our spiritual partnership.

- An enormous support system in the form of my attorney and the financial rescuer.

- Being forced to rise to forgiveness as the only acceptable, true solution to resolving the deeper issues of the party attacking me.

- Learning to make a clear separation between the evil done to me and the person causing it so I could denounce the evil, but not the person.

- Pole vaulting over any justification of hatred in my private consciousness.

- A radical strengthening of my healing practice to help others conquer oppression, helplessness, injustice, fear, and despair – and rise to the consciousness of spiritual abundance.

Imagine what I would be reporting to you today about this experience if my interpretation was recorded with anger, depletion, resentment, and helplessness – from a consciousness of poverty.

Do you think I would be co-authoring this book right now on liberating Magnificence?

The consciousness of abundance liberates our Magnificence

How can each of us live in the consciousness of abundance rather than the consciousness of poverty?

Through spiritual understanding.

The consciousness of abundance is anchored in this powerful idea:

A seed – or a divine idea – carries within itself everything needed for its complete fulfillment

A tiny seed already contains – within itself – everything necessary in order to develop a trunk and branches and leaves and become a tree, and even bear fruit. This same little seed also carries the entire longevity of the tree and all its years of flourishing and fruitfulness. This seed *already* *includes* its full outcome – the ability to provide shade, a place for animals to climb or perch, and perhaps food to support other life.

All this is contained *within* the tiny little seed – and even more. The seed also *includes* within itself the ability to multiply more seeds, and for those seeds also to multiply.

How's that for abundance?

That is exactly the way it works in the consciousness of abundance.

Each of us is exactly like a seed. We *already* include our completeness.

A key concept in the consciousness of abundance is that our substance is always *ideas*, not money. Ideas!

The consciousness of abundance focuses on the multiplication of ideas, not money

Every business, for example, represents an idea.

Every product or service begins with the *idea* for that product or service.

And within that idea – in its purest form – is included all the following: intelligence, support, provision, strength, recognition of its worth and value to others, intuitive marketing, integrity, protection, ability to attract and expand, energy, inspiration, vision, productivity, multiplication, and all else needed for its full expression of abundance.

That is what it means to have the consciousness of abundance. This may seem like radical thinking, but only because we are programmed to think in terms of poverty and lack.

We have highly developed habits of thinking in terms of what's missing rather than in terms of inherent completeness within us.

But these habits can be broken!

It is the nature
of the divine
to express abundance
in all things –
eternally

If you are facing a picture of lack right now, here are examples of affirmations you can use to stay awake to the consciousness of abundance – your genuine state.

Because I am spiritual, I *include* right now:

- Every right idea and its abundant supply of unlimited, outpouring of good.
- The clear vision of the idea and an understanding of how to take it forward to the next step and to all successive steps.
- The full ability to utilize this right idea in a practical way.

Here are even more affirmations of living in a consciousness of abundance:

- I can see that I am being divinely directed with the right plan to follow in order to develop and manifest the highest idea of good.
- I trust that this idea is totally integrated with my lifepath and includes all lessons I need to learn, as well as all talents that need to be expressed.
- I acknowledge that this idea carries within itself all it needs for its total

success and the ability to bless me with abundant supply – and all others as well.

- I will bring to this sacred idea my highest sense of honesty, fairness, and love that is required.

- I am grateful that this idea exempts me from fear, burden, and failure since I know this idea is divine and cannot fail.

- I will listen and follow angel thoughts which specialize in providing me with immediate and continual comfort, guidance, love, provision, inspiration, encouragement, help, understanding, and divine attraction to others who are divinely appointed to be part of this idea.

Gratitude is another sure path to abundance. One of the fastest ways to enter the consciousness of abundance is through the gate of gratitude.

Remembering the good you *already* include has a multiplying effect. This sacred exercise helps to awaken consciousness to its natural state of abundance.

Many of Shannon's clients have been healed of illness just from the medicine of making out a gratitude list. Others have been healed of severe financial difficulty by starting with this exercise.

Gratitude
opens us to
infinite abundance

Gratitude Exercise

List below 20 things you are *most* grateful for. Watch how your consciousness shifts from the beginning of the exercise to the end.

1. _____
2. _____
3. _____
4. _____
5. _____
6. _____
7. _____
8. _____
9. _____
10. _____
11. _____
12. _____
13. _____
14. _____
15. _____
16. _____
17. _____
18. _____
19. _____
20. _____

Magnificence Affirmation
Abundance

I acknowledge
that I include everything I need
– every idea –
right now
for the rest of eternity

I acknowledge
with overflowing gratitude
all the wonderful
ideas
of Mind & Love
that are supplying my life

I affirm
the infinitude and availability
of every divine idea
needed to support
all mankind

Loving Yourself with Magnificence!

Here is statement #14 again from the *Liberating Your Magnificence Quiz* in the appendix.

I live in the consciousness
of abundance, not lack.

What are the three most powerful things you can do to align your life with this statement?

1. _____

   _____

   _____

2. _____

   _____

   _____

3. _____

   _____

   _____

It is your
spiritual right
to live in the consciousness
of abundance

Magnificence Journal

What are you learning about the consciousness of abundance for your life?

_____

_____

_____

_____

_____

_____

_____

_____

_____

_____

_____

_____

_____

_____

Chapter 15

Live Without Fear
in the Assurance
of Love

It is your spiritual right to live without fear in the assurance of divine Love.

We all face fears:

- Fear of losing our health – or dying.
- Fear of losing a loved one.
- Fear of never being loved.
- Fear of being alone.
- Fear of losing a job.
- Fear of financial collapse.
- Fear of failing in a job.
- Fear for our children.
- Fear of being abused or mistreated.
- Fear of losing respect or dignity.
- Fear of never being what we dream to be.

Note this important point: in every case, fear is a perception of loss and separation from Love.

Michaelangelo's painting of creation in the Sistine Chapel shows God and man reaching out to touch each other – but short of touching by several inches.

How much sweeter if they had touched!

The divine touch is healing and reminds us that we have never been separated from Love

The truth is, we can never be separated from divine Love, our Source.

We need to remind ourselves that we are created by Love itself. Divine Love never lets go of us. The realization of our co-existence with divine Love calms, comforts, instructs, and lifts us to greater heights.

As we turn to divine Love daily and make decisions based on Love's guidance, then healing and spiritual growth naturally take place.

Divine Love dissolves fear

Here is an example from Shannon's life of healing fear with spiritual Love.

––––––––––

For over a year I struggled with a physical problem that brought a great deal of fear daily. There were few nights without a bombardment of fearful thoughts.

During the worst of it, I recall a night that I slept in the guest bedroom. I awoke in a panic and was so terrified that my body was quivering. All my symptoms had returned. Fear was alarming. As is sometimes the case with intense fear, we are tempted to believe in the worst.

I knew I could go in the next room and wake Scott. He and I had prayed about this problem so I felt supported by all the wonderful prayers we had shared both together and independently. Still, however, the fears persisted.

I lay there, quiver and all, and asked God to give me the thoughts I needed for healing. I lay there for hours – listening for the assurance of God's presence.

Far from passive, I was actively engaged in feeling close to divine Love. I reminded myself that I was leaning on Love to tell me what to think and how to go forward with healing. I was doing what I had done for the past twenty years – relying on divine Love to teach, heal, inspire, and direct my life.

Then it unfolded. My prayer was answered – not with words but with these thoughts of spiritual Love:

- I am not alone.
- I am not separate from God.
- I am at one with divine Love.

I felt it.

That moment has forever changed my outlook on fear. I felt the presence and assurance of divine Love. It was solid.

This moment was a powerful turning point because fear was faced and vastly lessened. Based on what I learned about the presence of Love, the physical problem was healed.

As a spiritual healer, I grew enormously from this experience. I learned how to take a stand so radical and powerful that it took me to a whole new level of healing.

***Each of us
can turn to the Source
of all comfort
and experience Love's
healing presence***

You are probably familiar with the acronym for fear – **F**alse **E**vidence *Appearing* **R**eal.

We remove fear by seeing it as an illusion and letting in the light of Love. It is helpful to categorize fear as a belief, an illusion, or a false perception of reality. Fear is not "out there," but is based on a false perception that reality is void of divine Love.

Since fear thoughts are pervasive, they need to be addressed daily. Here's how we can address fear and dissolve it:

- Think of fear as a false perception.
- Recognize that our need to be free of fear is a spiritual *right*.
- Lean on Love's comforting and healing thoughts to calm us.
- Allow Love's presence to replace fears and meet our needs.

> *Fear disappears*
> *with the understanding*
> *that fear is simply*
> *a belief*
> *in the absence*
> *of Love*

Spiritual trust and listening opens us to a consciousness of the presence and assurance of divine Love. As we open to this consciousness, we simultaneously give up fear.

This powerful spiritual awakening to Love's power to dissolve fear is occurring on a world scale. World belief in fear is being replaced by a higher understanding of the all-presence of divine Love.

This is what the liberation of your Magnificence is all about. We are all learning to think without fear!

For example, what would happen in your life if your Magnificence was unleashed without any fear? Go ahead, kick back all your mental boundaries and imagine your life without any fear.

It is your spiritual right to live without fear in the assurance of Love

Spiritual reasoning strengthens our trust in Love and diminishes fear in every area of our lives – health, relationships, and abundance.

It would be naïve to think that an occasional prayer would be sufficient to keep us awake to Love's allness. We need to change our habits of thought so that our consciousness becomes Love-centered rather than fear-centered.

Rather than thinking of Love as something we need to add to our lives, we need to think of divine Love as a constant presence with us. We are incapable of being separated from Love.

By remembering Love as the Creator of all existence – as a caring and powerful presence in our lives – we experience the consciousness of Love and it's assurance. This heals us of fear.

As we address fear in any area of our thinking, we simultaneously dissolve fear in all areas of our lives. Being faithful to spiritual thinking brings immense comfort and allows our fear index to steadily decrease. Continuing to contemplate our relationship with divine Love, we become enveloped in its presence and fear fades until it vanishes.

Healing of fear always occurs when we wake to Love's ever-presence

Magnificence Affirmation

The
Assurance & Presence
of Love

*I live
at one with
divine assurance
because
Love is always with me
and guiding me*

*I live
in an eternal succession
of divine moments
of Love's comfort and assurance
where fear is unknown*

*The same Love
that is directing my life
is also dissolving
all fear
for all mankind*

Loving Yourself with Magnificence!

Here is statement #15 again from the *Liberating Your Magnificence Quiz* in the appendix.

**I live without fear
in the assurance of divine Love.**

What are the three most powerful things you can do to align your life with this statement?

1. _____
   _____
   _____

2. _____
   _____
   _____

3. _____
   _____
   _____

*It is your
spiritual right
to live
without fear
in the assurance of Love*

Magnificence Journal

What are you learning about healing fear with the assurance of divine Love?

_____

_____

_____

_____

_____

_____

_____

_____

_____

_____

_____

_____

_____

_____

Chapter 16

Dissolve
Anger with
Unconditional Love

Anger imprisons us.

Love liberates us.

Think of it. You finally find your lifepath. You start moving towards your dreams. Your light begins to shine. And then anger surfaces.

All progress stops. All energy needed for forward Magnificence-thrust is suddenly rerouted to vent anger – or recover from it.

Anger is devastating and destructive. It's a poison that drains us.

If your car was headed towards a highly toxic waste site, the moment you became aware of it, you would steer the car in the opposite direction.

It's the same way with anger. So look for the posted signs that say "Toxic Anger" and go in the opposite direction.

Head for Love.

***All roads
away from anger
lead home
to Love***

Love dissolves anger.

As a defender of your Magnificence, recognize that anger causes irritation, hate, and, in some cases, even murder. Rise with spiritual authority that knows, declares, and proves that divine Love is always more powerful than anger.

Is anger your real *substance* – the *substance* of your Life Message?

Of course not.

Your Life Message is anchored in Love.

But how can we handle anger? What can we do, for example, when we get angry at someone?

Rise to Love – swiftly!

Instantly recognize that anger is not only destructive – but that the person it will most harm – even attempt to destroy – is *you!*

Swiftly make the separation between the person (whether you or another) and the anger. Depersonalize it. The sooner this is done the sooner the healing can come.

Here is a real-life example of the power of love to heal anger instantly:

We have a totally organic garden and yard surrounding our home. It took over three years of patient and joyful work to create an environment where flowers, trees, and vegetables flourish in rich, organic soil with no toxins or chemicals whatsoever. It looks and smells – to us and the hummingbirds, butterflies, and earthworms – like heaven.

Well, while writing this book, we had a massive ant infestation on our property. So Shannon called a pest control company and, after many conversations about organic gardening, felt comfortable with their assurances that they would use an organic-compatible treatment which would not affect the multitude of life in our garden.

Here's what happened – in Shannon's words:

On the day scheduled for treatment, the company sent out a new employee who sprinkled a deadly chemical poison all over the yard – everywhere!   He even dutifully left a slip under the door to confirm what he'd done.

I was heartbroken.

My three years of work to develop this wonderful bio-diversity of life in our yard was destroyed in fifteen minutes.

An apology would not change the damage.

When I felt myself going into anger, I remembered that anger was just another word for toxin. I immediately decided to stop the anger. It was a choice. I thought to myself:

- Why depart from my lifepath of love?
- Why engage in thinking totally foreign to my spirituality?

Then I thought of the new employee who had done it and removed from my thinking all anger and condemnation. I wanted, more than anything else, to live free of anger and to be able to flow with love.

I made the separation. I declared – to myself – this man's innate innocence and goodness and united myself with divine Love that understands and forgives.

When we separate evil
from a person
we open the door to
forgiveness

I sent a letter to the company telling them what had happened and the owner sent a beautiful letter of apology in return. Then I went the extra mile and sent him a letter accepting his apology and telling him that, on a scale between one and ten, his apology was a ten – which it was.

Now be sure to see the big picture here.

Anger is always just a *thought* attempting to enter and dominate our consciousness.

When we detach an anger-thought from a person and rise into our native consciousness of Love, we are instantly freed to move forward.

The garden experience is not just a story of overcoming anger. I was expressing my right to liberate my Magnificence and stay in the consciousness of divine Love.

My stand for liberation that embraced everyone brought forth the owner's Magnificence in the form of honest compassion and an apology.

A
win over anger
is a win
for everyone

What about someone who is angry at you?

We all know what it is like to be screamed at. Our Magnificence energy drops instantly to zero and our defense energies are exhausted as we cope with fear, defend ourselves, or retreat in emotional withdrawal. Anger is totally counterproductive to growth, happiness, or Magnificence.

Anger is really a *belief* that evil has power, wants to punish, and has power to punish.

Shannon often has calls from people who are in relationships where unkindness or anger are tearing apart emotions – and families.

Why don't these people stand up to such anger-riddled relationships – or leave? The one thing these struggling hearts often have in common is their sympathy with the anger:

- They tend to make excuses for the other person's anger.
- They tell themselves it will pass and it's not that bad.
- They tell themselves they made it through the last bout with anger and they can get through it again.
- They tell themselves that their loved one cannot help it and anger is a part of their character.
- They tell themselves maybe it will get better.
- They practice helplessness and refuse to take a stand because they are convinced of their inability to win – or their fear that they might lose their "loved" one.

Please memorize this scenario as the picture of lose-lose, no liberation, and zero Magnificence.

Ask yourself:

- Do I want to continue to pay for another person's problem?
- Am I willing to step out of the darkness of anger attacks in order to live a life of liberation?
- How much do I want to live my Magnificence?

Shannon understands this dilemma because she was forced to rise out of anger into liberation and forgiveness in her own previous marriage. Here are her words:

When my marriage fell apart, I felt totally abandoned. A month later, my ex-husband came by the house in a limousine with a girlfriend – to pick up our teenage daughter for a Christmas party. I spent the night alone in tears and great anger.

I prayed with all my heart to remove the anger – and I didn't stop that night. From that moment on, I took a vehement stand to dissolve the anger. Sometimes I woke during the night in a rage and diligently prayed to see the anger removed from me.

Finally, I began to look at both my husband and his girlfriend as they were when they were babies – pure and innocent, harmless and good. I thought of how I would feel if I were the mother of either of them. I practiced Mother love.

I fought hard for my right to be separate from anger and hate. And I won. They won. I carried no hard feelings and to this day I wish them well.

Over a year later, my mental stand to stay in the consciousness of Love's Magnificence led me to Scott and our marriage of unconditional love.

Unconditional love always takes us to greater Magnificence

Is unconditional love really possible?
Of course it is!
But first, we have to *conceive* that it is possible.

**You are not likely to
experience love
at a
higher level
than you can conceive**

Here is a good example:

A man from another state called Scott one morning. He didn't know Scott, but asked if they could talk. The man said that he and his wife had just finished reading *The Love You Deserve*, but that he was very afraid he was going to lose his wife – and he didn't want that to happen.

Scott asked why she might leave.

He said because he had expressed a lot of anger through the years and did not believe she could ever forgive him for the way he had treated their children.

He added, though, that things were better during the last several weeks and even the kids had noticed. He said he was trying to be less angry.

Almost spontaneously, but with great compassion for all of them, Scott said: "What your wife and kids deserve is not *less* anger, but *no* anger."

There was a quietness and then his words, "I never even thought of that as a possibility."

Healing always begins with a higher thought.

**A
consciousness of Love
is permanently
free
from anger**

Magnificence Affirmation

Love
Dissolves Anger

*Because I am
the manifestation of Love
I have power to thwart anger
at once*

*I live
in the liberation of infinite Love
which cannot be
contaminated with any
toxic thought
or feeling*

*As Love's expression,
I represent forgiveness
every moment*

*As Love's infinite nature,
I represent
freedom & liberation
for all mankind*

Loving Yourself with Magnificence!

Here is statement #16 again from the *Liberating Your Magnificence Quiz* in the appendix.

I live in the consciousness of Love that dissolves all anger.

What are the three most powerful things you can do to align your life with this statement?

1. _____

   _____

   _____

2. _____

   _____

   _____

3. _____

   _____

   _____

*It is your
spiritual right
to live in the consciousness
of Love, not anger*

Magnificence Journal

How is divine Love dissolving anger in your most inward consciousness?

_____

_____

_____

_____

_____

_____

_____

_____

_____

_____

_____

_____

_____

_____

Chapter 17

Break Out
of Time & Age into
Eternity Consciousness

Let's shift into eternity consciousness.

Eternity is not a destination. Eternity is present reality – a state of consciousness that is open to infinite good and sees Light.

You are living in eternity right now.

The only question is: "Are you conscious of living in eternity?"

We don't realize the extent to which our thinking is bogged down in time and age. How often do these thoughts dominate your consciousness?

- I'm too old.
- It's too late.
- I'm running out of time.
- I'm worried about my body.
- I'll never get it all done.
- It would take a million years to reach my dreams.

All these thoughts of time and age lead to the same place – to death, not life.

It is time
to rise out of
the paradigm of death
into the consciousness of
eternal life

Let us rise to true Magnificence and declare the truth – it is time for us to stop dying.

Think of death as an illusion, just like the horizon. If you were on a ship traveling towards the horizon, when would you reach the horizon?

Never! The horizon only appears to be a destination, but it is unobtainable, since it is an illusion.

If someone you love gets on a ship and moves toward the horizon, the ship may eventually disappear over the horizon. But the person on board would not be aware of arriving on the horizon.

If that loved one could speak to us, they'd tell us of their current life and joy, their love, peace, and progress and what is making them smile.

Scott's mother practiced and taught the consciousness of eternity and spiritual joy so clearly to Scott that, when she passed on, Scott felt no grief – because her *substance* was so evident and still so present.

Far from ending their relationship, his close bond of love with his mother not only continued, but has expanded as her *substance* continues to radiate its Magnificence. For example, her words of spiritual wisdom, so often spoken to Scott, continue registering with Magnificence and new meanings.

Substance, not *form*.

Your material body is not who you really are. It is only the present *form* of your life, not your *substance*.

Think of the three people you most admire:

1. _____

2. _____

3. _____

Is it because of their *form* – their looks?

Probably not! You admire their *substance* – the qualities and consciousness they express. Their contribution is eternal. This is their Magnificence!

The
reality
of our lives
is that our substance
is eternal

Let us demolish death in another *form* as well – the form that suggests our *identity* is dying. This is the fear that would cry:

- What if my true worth and gifts are never recognized, expressed, or seen?
- What if my value never gets out in the open?
- What if there is not enough time?
- What if I am too old?
- What if I never have the opportunity?

Eternity consciousness instantly comes to our defense and aligns us to divine reality. There can be no loss of identity because who we are cannot be lessened or erased.

Our *substance* is inherently eternal.

Here is Shannon's story of facing down the challenge of identity-death:

When I suddenly became single after many years of marriage, it felt like the bottom fell out of my life. I was afraid that my life was over – that all my hopes and dreams would never be expressed or known. I felt unwanted, unloved, and expendable – marked "void and ready for extinction."   It felt like my identity was dying.

This *forced* me to rise to eternity consciousness. As I rose in rebellion against these thoughts, I claimed my identity to be in total oneness with divine Love. I learned several huge lessons as I thought of my life united with Love:

- Divine Love cannot be invaded by fear or loss. Love is impregnable and will never cease. Love is eternal, the only real substance.

- My identity as the expression of divine Love means that I can never be separated from Love – never be unexpressed, never be extinct.

Eternity consciousness constantly re-anchors us in our infinite Magnificence

All of us are faced with enormous challenges to the liberation of our Magnificence.

Don't be surprised by massive resistance within your consciousness to eternity consciousness. We are all taking gigantic leaps forward together spiritually. We are:

- Sending death into oblivion.
- Saying "No!" to long-established *belief habits* that have anchored our thinking in birth, decay, and death.
- Claiming our identity – our true body – to be the *substance* of our Magnificence.
- Leaving the paradigm of restricted, confining, finite, and unliberated consciousness.

- Shifting into a whole new way of thinking and living – into eternity consciousness.

- Exploring our new world of eternity and learning to embrace infinity.

- Ascending into Light and Love.

As you make this journey to your new mental home of eternity consciousness, here are some hints:

1. **Practice eternity consciousness.** Challenge every thought that enters your consciousness and accept only those that have eternal substance. For example, the thought "I'm tired" does not gain entrance. The thought "I'm the expression of inexhaustible Love" does.

2. **Replace time and age habits with eternity habits.** For example, think of "stress," not as the overwhelm of too much to do in too short a time, but as the *wrong consciousness* for your life. Allow yourself to rise from the consciousness of limitation to eternity consciousness. Let yourself enjoy divine Love's view of what needs to be done. Be at one with Love's effortless action.

3. **Think eternally.** For example, what will be your biggest contribution *in eternity*? Go ahead. Allow yourself to think without limits.

Eternity consciousness
reveals our true
Magnificence

Affirmation

Eternity Consciousness

Because
I am at one with Light
I am liberated
from time and age
and live
in eternity

I know myself
– my substance –
to be
the expression
of inexhaustible
Love

I see my life
as the unfolding
of divine ideas
spilling out in vast unending
creativity

Loving Yourself with Magnificence!

Here is statement #17 again from the *Liberating Your Magnificence Quiz* in the appendix.

I live outside of time and age in eternity consciousness.

What are the three most powerful things you can do to align your life with this statement?

1. _____

   _____

   _____

2. _____

   _____

   _____

3. _____

   _____

   _____

It is your
spiritual right
to live in
eternity consciousness

Magnificence Journal

What are you learning – for yourself – about eternity consciousness?

_____

_____

_____

_____

_____

_____

_____

_____

_____

_____

_____

_____

_____

_____

Chapter 18

Move
Past Rejection
to Higher Unfoldment

Rejection stings our soul – sends our identity into shock and reeling.

On the surface, rejection causes us to feel hurt and angry – sometimes for a long time.

More significantly, deep within our inner self, rejection causes us to think: "I'm obviously not worthy. What's wrong with me? I thought I was valuable."

All of this is a trap.

Not the trap of rejection, but the trap of not understanding what is truly taking place in the unfoldment of our unique identity and spiritual purpose.

Here is the truth that liberates Magnificence:

Rejection,
by its very nature of
closing a door,
forces us to open consciousness
to a higher unfoldment
of Magnificence

And oh how we resist this blessing!

The rejection shock when Shannon's earlier marriage ended felt like a giant train wreck. Yet, looking back, she can *now* see that, at the very moment she felt she was in a train wreck, divine Love was actually lifting her out of a relationship that was oppressive.

If that door had not closed on Shannon, we would not be married today nor enjoying our work together as "The Love Team." And this book would not exist!

And look what happened in Scott's life:

Many years ago, an organization where he had worked for 10 years let him go after his department was dissolved. This closing door forced him to reassess his identity.

That "rejection" resulted in the following unfoldment of Magnificence:

- Scott moved to California and began an entire new occupation from scratch – real estate – and rose to the top 5% of all Prudential agents in the nation.

- Scott was forced to confront and become liberated from a marriage that wasn't working – for either of them.

- Scott met and married Shannon – his soulmate and spiritual partner.

- Scott's self-worth jumped from dirt to divinity. He began living out from Soul, not doubt.

- Scott discovered and began radiating the core of his substance – the Magnificence he had to offer the universe.

- Scott wrote, with Shannon's enormous support, the widely-acclaimed book, *The Love You Deserve*. And now this book.

Here is the key lesson:

These opening doors to blessing are all very clear – looking *backwards* in time! We all have 20-20 vision looking backwards.

The Magnificence expertise we need is to look *forward* with vision!

> *If you really*
> ***REALLY***
> *love yourself,*
> ***move past rejection like a swift wind***
> ***and open your receptivity***
> ***to bigger doors***
> ***and trust***
> ***that they are there***

Such trust is not blind faith but spiritual understanding. It is the deep assurance within your innermost trust in Soul that the *substance* of your identity will open doors for your Magnificence to shine.

Jack Canfield and Mark Victor Hanson, the co-authors of the *Chicken Soup for the Soul* books, bring this powerful declaration to rejection:

"Next!"

And they move on to bigger doors.

Their first book was rejected by multiple publishers. Today their many books have swept the world.

"Next!"

Rejection rehearsal would have you mulling the closed doors over and over and over.

Such rejection-stuck thinking is a denial of your Magnificence, a direct assault on your spirituality and divine identity.

Your #1 job in handling rejection is to mentally walk away from closed doors and stay focused on your divine substance and spiritual purpose. Open your consciousness to the doors of blessing that Love is even now unfolding as your higher path.

Let your highest spiritual consciousness align with this truth:

> **Nothing
> in the universe
> can stop your Magnificence
> from unfolding to completeness
> because your
> Life Message
> is your
> divine destiny –
> divinity expressing you!**

Magnificence Affirmation

Higher Unfolding

*I am the
very unfolding
of God's Magnificence*

*I am able
to move past rejection
because my life is open
to Spirit's highest unfolding
of my Magnificence*

*Infinite
Mind & Love
are even now guiding me
to Spirit's open doors &
ushering in the full expression
of my Magnificence*

Loving Yourself with Magnificence!

Here is statement #18 again from the *Liberating Your Magnificence Quiz* in the appendix.

I quickly move past rejection
to a higher unfoldment of Magnificence.

What are the three most powerful things you can do to align your life with this statement?

1. _____
   _____
   _____

2. _____
   _____
   _____

3. _____
   _____
   _____

*It is your
spiritual right
to live in the assurance
of Love's
open doors*

Magnificence Journal

How are you moving from rejection towards a higher unfolding of your Magnificence?

_____

_____

_____

_____

_____

_____

_____

_____

_____

_____

_____

_____

_____

_____

Chapter 19

Shift Swiftly
from Overwhelm to
Liberation

We have come a long way together in the freeing of your Magnificence.

We have faced and challenged doubt, guilt, lack, fear, anger, time, age, and rejection. That's a lot to be grateful for!

Now it's time for one last powerful skill – a skill designed to guarantee no retreat and to quickly defeat attacks of overwhelm.

Each of us, no matter how successful we have been in defeating the challenges to the liberation of our Magnificence, have days – or even weeks – when we feel overwhelmed.

Sometimes fear-storms, doubt-clouds, lack-attacks, anger-blasts, guilt-relapses, and time-drain seem to attack us from all directions simultaneously.

How can we stay on top – in the consciousness of liberation?

We
defeat all attacks
on our Magnificence
by staying alert
&
responding to attacks
instantaneously!

Pilots, for example, have a multitude of instruments facing them in the cockpit – altitude, airspeed, rate of climb or descent, compass heading, fuel, flaps, and on and on. And it only takes failure in *one* of these critical areas to crash.

That's why pilots *scan* their instruments rapidly and repeatedly in a sweep of the mental eyes – to see the BIG picture all at once and respond to trouble *immediately*!

Scott, like most rookie private pilots, remembers learning this lesson early on. On one early flight in his training, he was proud to be holding the plane on a steady compass heading, but was finding it hard to keep the plane at a consistent altitude. So Scott fixated on the altitude instrument with great determination to succeed. And he nailed it – total success! He was holding a steady altitude.

But when he looked up from the instrument and looked out the cockpit window, the plane – although now holding its altitude perfectly – was flying in a circle. He was no longer on course.

It takes practice to learn to scan all the instruments at once – to look for critical needs, correct them instantly, and then go back to an overall scan. This is the skill that will keep you in Magnificence consciousness.

Let's take a Magnificence scan of your life right now. The next page provides a big picture approach to scanning your Magnificence status. Scan the page quickly to detect any "Red Alert" areas.

Get ready. Scan!

Magnificence
Scan Check

As fast as you can, scan the *Liberating Your Magnificence* instrument cluster below and identify the "Red Alert" areas that need *instant* attention.

Cherishing My Magnificence
Status

Giving myself solitude	Good	Fair	Red Alert
Defending my wholeness	Good	Fair	Red Alert
Not comparing to others	Good	Fair	Red Alert
Surrounded with honoring	Good	Fair	Red Alert
Welcoming expansion	Good	Fair	Red Alert
Living in *NOW*	Good	Fair	Red Alert
Trusting Love	Good	Fair	Red Alert
Using spiritual affirmations	Good	Fair	Red Alert

Freeing My Magnificence
Status

Living in Soul, not doubt	Good	Fair	Red Alert
No guilt/innocence/freedom	Good	Fair	Red Alert
Abundance consciousness	Good	Fair	Red Alert
Living without fear	Good	Fair	Red Alert
Dissolving anger with Love	Good	Fair	Red Alert
Living outside time & age	Good	Fair	Red Alert
Saying "Next!" to rejection	Good	Fair	Red Alert
Shifting quickly to liberation	Good	Fair	Red Alert

Radiating My Magnificence
Status

One step per day to dreams	Good	Fair	Red Alert
Praising with Magnificence	Good	Fair	Red Alert
Exuding joy	Good	Fair	Red Alert
Living in infinite possibilities	Good	Fair	Red Alert
Loving unconditionally	Good	Fair	Red Alert
Liberating others	Good	Fair	Red Alert

It may seem hard to scan this page quickly, but it gets much easier once you truly understand the importance of each key. Think of this as "Magnificence expertise" and decide to become an expert at scanning your entire cockpit of instruments in one rapid sweep.

Can you imagine what such a scan does for the health of your Magnificence?

For example, let's say you're moving along, having a productive day, and then someone makes a small comment that causes you to feel doubt.

What often happens is that we continue our day, but something doesn't feel right. Our spirits begin sinking. We can't put our finger on it. The day has been good overall, but our productivity just isn't there. We keep going forward, but with less zip.

If, however, you were routinely completing a Magnificence scan, what would happen differently?

During your scan, your doubt instrument would beep "Red Alert" and all your spiritual and mental energy would *instantly* focus on getting your doubt status back on line – immediately.

The potential solutions are infinite. You might:

- Quickly review the chapter on doubt.
- Get the doubt out in the open with a friend who honors you and will lift you back to Magnificence.
- Laugh at the doubt as a *false belief* trying to intrude and knock your life off course.
- Make powerful spiritual affirmations of your oneness with divine Mind and annihilate the doubt on the spot.

What is thrilling about becoming an expert at scanning your Magnificence instruments, is that *you* take total charge of the liberation of your Magnificence.

You are the pilot. You have control.

This may seem hard when you are at a point of breakdown, overwhelm, or tears in your life, but even then, learn to take control of yourself as the pilot in command.

Here is a revealing pilot story – in Scott's words:

––––––

In one of my early solo flights – flying for the first time without an instructor – I was required to make a flight of at least 25 nautical miles, land at another airstrip, and then return home. I must have spent five hours planning for this short journey.

Well, there I was, flying alone above the world in this small 2-seater plane with no one in the other seat (where my instructor used to be). It was thrilling but also scary.

When I reached the destination airfield (according to my map and instruments), I looked down but saw nothing but green countryside – no runway anywhere!

Looking out my side window, I was so focused on finding that runway that the plane started to tilt. That was easy to correct, but since the plane was continuing along at 150 mph, there was little hope of easily spotting the runway.

I realized then what a mistake I had made to select such a tiny airport runway located in the all-green countryside rather than one near a lake or some highly visible landmark – but that realization didn't help at that moment.

As much as I wanted to simply pull my plane out of the sky, completely stop, look at a map, and gather my senses, the reality was that I was alone, flying at 150 mph, and had no idea where that airport runway was.

That moment taught me a great lesson:

No matter how futile a situation seems,
we can always focus,
regain composure,
&
make intelligent decisions

What other choice was there? Either I would pull myself together and make an intelligent decision – or I would eventually crash.

I gathered my thoughts, decided to forget about finding this landing strip, and return home to my own little airfield – before any further disorientation.

And let me tell you. Can you imagine the feeling of relief in *f i n a l l y* touching down back at home?

When my instructor asked, "How did it go?" I humorously pretended to be a pilot making an announcement to the passengers: "This is your pilot speaking. We were unable to find our destination airport so we've returned home. Hope you enjoyed the flight!"

I think of this story often when faced with overwhelm or crisis. We always have the ability to pull ourselves back into Magnificence. It's a mental choice. We are never without solutions.

Welcome
to the cockpit
of your Magnificence

Magnificence Affirmation

Scanning
for Magnificence

*I am able
to scan the status
of my Magnificence
with the speed and insight of
divine Light*

*I am able
to solve all problems
that confront my liberation
with the power
of Mind*

*I see
and affirm
that all mankind
is right now flying in the arms
of Love*

Loving Yourself with Magnificence!

Here is statement #19 again from the *Liberating Your Magnificence Quiz.*

I shift swiftly from overwhelm to liberation.

What are the three most powerful things you can do to align your life with this statement?

1. _____

   _____

   _____

2. _____

   _____

   _____

3. _____

   _____

   _____

It is your
spiritual right
to rise swiftly from overwhelm
to liberation

Magnificence Journal

What are you learning about rising swiftly from overwhelm to liberation?

_____

_____

_____

_____

_____

_____

_____

_____

_____

_____

_____

_____

_____

_____

Stage 4

Radiate
Your
Magnificence

Chapter 20

Take One Step
Each Day
to
Liberate
Your Magnificence

Welcome to utter bliss.

As you step into this final section of the book, you are entering a new era of light in your life called:

Radiating
Your Magnificence!

- Letting your Magnificence out of hiding.
- Glowing, shining, illumining, lighting up, shimmering, blazing.
- Exuding your Magnificence.
- Enlightening, inspiring, elucidating, revealing.
- Broadcasting, circulating, dispersing, disseminating, divulging.
- Living at one with your Magnificence.
- *Being* your Magnificence!

Think of the beauty and intensity of one single, tiny beam of light shimmering through a crack into a dark room. Or the majesty and inspiring power of a single candle shining in darkness.

Spiritual Light in our lives is not measured by size, but by *substance* – the illumination of Love and Soul.   Lives of Magnificence are like those single beams and candles, inspiring and uplifting the entire universe.

You are one of those beams of Light.

So is all mankind.

We face each new day of our life of Magnificence, not with fear and doubt and heavy schedules, but with a consciousness of radiant Magnificence.

Not Magnificence tomorrow.

Magnificence now.

Even
the smallest step
towards radiating your Magnificence
is like
a beam of divine Light
illuminating your heart with joy
and lifting you
to the heart of your
Magnificence

The power of a single step is awesome.

Radiating your Magnificence in the smallest of ways is like a single spark that ignites your life passion.

Let's talk about that single step.

Think again about where this book started and what you have discovered about your Life Message.

In fact, use the following box to jot down again –
in one sentence – your current best version of your
Life Message.

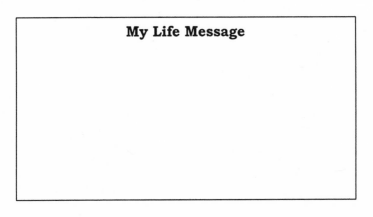

For us, we'd still come back to our message:

*Bringing all mankind into
the heart of Love*

Now, think of the arguments that would prevent
you from liberating your Magnificence *today*:

- My schedule today is totally full. I have
  no room at all for my Life Message.
- I'm just not mentally prepared to express
  Magnificence today.
- I couldn't possibly tackle such a gigantic
  task today.
- I admit that this is a good idea and I'll do
  it when I finish my tasks, chores, and
  responsibilities.

Why do you suppose that time management
courses never go out of style? For one, because our
days are getting *more* complex and *more* packed, not
less.

The solution, however, is so simple that you might underestimate its power to liberate Magnificence.

The solution to liberating your Magnificence is to take one tiny step – each day

That's right – *one* step *each* day. The key is to make that one step so small that you'd have to laugh at yourself for not doing it.

For example, writing this book seemed an overwhelming task in the midst of a sea of responsibilities that never seemed to end, but here are the tiny steps that paved the way to Magnificence:

- Labeling an empty file folder "Magnificence."
- Creating a blank document in the computer called "Magnificence."
- Opening the blank document and typing in a few chapter titles.
- Buying a pack of 4x6 cards.
- Deciding mentally to write 25 twelve-page books rather than one 300-page book.
- Opening the "Magnificence" document in the computer, exalting in finding that there was actually something there, and adding a few more ideas.
- Printing out the chapter titles and holding it in our hands like a new baby.
- Driving along the California coast while visiting our daughter and writing down one main idea for each chapter on a 4x6 card.

- Falling in love with the potential of our book.
- Writing out the content of chapter one together on a paper placemat at a restaurant.
- Writing for a brief period each day.

That's what we call small steps – yet you are now holding the result. Think of how happy we felt taking each one of those little steps. Because these steps were so small, we were lifted out of a consciousness of time to a consciousness of Magnificence unfolding in eternity.

One single step mushrooms into Magnificence.

But how, you might ask, will we ever tackle our Life Message – bringing all mankind into the heart of Love? Isn't that just too big for small steps?

Absolutely not. Look at the choices open to us:

- We can smile at each other when we wake up and say "I love you."
- We can smile with joy at a neighbor when we pick up our newspaper in the early morning.
- We can go to work and *see* the depth of the people behind the tasks – their dignity and worth – and love them.
- We can silently affirm the Magnificence of every person on this planet.

Each small, individual step
towards
Magnificence
carries all the power of its
completeness

Small Steps to Your Magnificence

List 5 *tiny* steps that you could take to liberate your Magnificence:

1. _____

2. _____

3. _____

4. _____

5. _____

List 5 more valuable steps that you could take to liberate your Magnificence:

1. _____

2. _____

3. _____

4. _____

5. _____

Never underestimate the power of a single step

Magnificence Affirmation

The Power of
One Step

*I am able
to take one step to
Magnificence
today
because Love
is continually unfolding
my spiritual purpose*

*I am able
to radiate Magnificence
today
because I am
at one with
Soul's Magnificence*

*I treasure
each step
that mankind
is taking today
to
liberate Magnificence*

Loving Yourself with Magnificence!

Here is statement #20 again from the *Liberating Your Magnificence Quiz* in the appendix.

**I take one step every day to
liberate my Magnificence.**

What are the three most powerful things you can do to align your life with this statement?

1. _____

   _____

   _____

2. _____

   _____

   _____

3. _____

   _____

   _____

*It is your
spiritual right
to
radiate
your Magnificence*

Magnificence Journal

How is your Magnificence emerging, expressing, and radiating itself?

_____

_____

_____

_____

_____

_____

_____

_____

_____

_____

_____

_____

_____

_____

_____

_____

Chapter 21

Praise
Generously

Praise lifts us to Magnificence.

In the presence of someone who tells us we are wonderful, admires our ideas, washes us with praise, cheers us on with enthusiastic confidence, loves us, and acknowledges our worth, our whole identity rises to Magnificence.

Magnificence – by its very nature – includes infinite, unconditional, oceans of praising Love. Why would we ever *give* less than this to the universe? As we advance to the final stage of radiating our Magnificence, we have no other choice but to be masters of generous praise.

Your Magnificence cannot be contained. It must be radiated to be real. Each breath of praise you *give* to the universe expands your Magnificence into radiant reality.

In this final stage of the liberation of your Magnificence, we discover a great truth:

Generous praising
liberates
our
own Magnificence

Here is a revealing exercise:

Who are the three people who praise you the most?

1. _____

2. _____

3. _____

How do you *feel* in their presence?

Praise uplifts our entire being!

Who are the three people who most withhold praise from you?

1. _____

2. _____

3. _____

How do you *feel* in their presence?

Lack of praise devastates our hearts!

On a scale of 1 to 10, how generously do *you* praise?

    1 2 3 4 5 6 7 8 9 10
Not at all   Some   Always

The liberation of your Magnificence is calling you to rise – *at a minimum* – to a nine. Anything less will hold back the full liberation of *your* Magnificence. And why not be a 10!

How can we possibly liberate our own Magnificence while we ignore the hearts of those right next to us?

If you are not an *abundant* giver of praise, let those days be washed away and forever gone from your identity. You have entered a higher platform of living where the full liberation of your Magnificence radiates praise as easily as you breathe.

Let your life be a trail of generous praise to the entire universe – and the universe includes *every individual* in the path of your expanding life.

The
liberation of your Magnificence
demands
the infinite unleashing
of floodtides
of praise – from you!

Here is a shining example of someone who praises with excellence.

Helice Bridges, "the First Lady of Acknowledgment," has carried a dream in her heart for the last twenty years – that each person on our planet deserves to be acknowledged and praised for the difference he or she makes to the universe.

Her dream gave birth to a blue ribbon ceremony that lasts about a minute – but what a minute! She first acknowledges another person's special worth and dreams – and then places a blue ribbon on their heart which says:

Who I Am Makes A Difference™

Through her efforts, blue ribbons have already been placed on more than 10 million hearts. As those in her presence have felt the power of her words and caught the spark of her enthusiasm for praising, her dream has expanded into a world vision of everyone on our planet turning to each other with such praise and acknowledgement.

Catch the spark!

Let this power of praise flow into your life like a tidal wave of Love. Begin to imagine the vast rewards in your life of becoming an expert at praising. Here are some guidelines to help you praise with Magnificence:

1. Praise divine Love, the Source of all being. Acknowledge your oneness with divine Love that enables your praise to flow openly and freely from Love's unconditional nature.

2. Release all judgment and criticism and rise to the consciousness of praise. Rise into the consciousness of infinite Love that is the *substance* of your Magnificence. Rise into pure giving.

3. Let your heart overflow with a desire to see and acknowledge Magnificence in every single person you meet on your path today. Let your praise always be genuine, and don't be a withholder of love. Your praise has the power to heal and uplift lives.

4. Praise first. Let your standard be to always praise three things before you ever offer a suggestion or judgment. This step alone will revolutionize your relationships.

5. Let your praise come out from deep within your heart and everything you have learned about Magnificence.

6. Be generous in your praising. Let the words keep flowing out until you see the smile of genuine reception that says, "I truly feel loved. Thank you."

7. Be dependable in your praise. Let your life be one where others know in advance that they will be acknowledged as valuable. Don't let anyone wonder whether you will be loving today – or whether you are in the mood to praise.

8. Praise strangers. When you flow by all those on your lifepath, recognize the good they are expressing and give them a compliment: "Thanks for your great service." "You have a beautiful smile." "That's a great dog of yours." You'll be astounded at the results.

9. Praise *yourself* in the inner heart of your Magnificence for taking such a radical stand for Love. You deserve to be praised!

10. Observe how your radiating of praise liberates your own Magnificence.

The habit of
praising & acknowledging
keeps us centered in
Magnificence

In fact, we'd like to end this chapter praising you.

We honor your commitment to liberating your Magnificence. The very fact that you are reading the words in this chapter shows your openness to growth, your humility, your commitment to excellence, and the love in your heart.

We cherish your dreams. It does not matter whether we know you personally. We are all united.

Magnificence unites us.

Every moment you praise another person, you are helping us in our mission to bring all mankind into the heart of Love. So we praise *you* right now for every thought and word of praise that has ever radiated from your being.

Thank you for your Magnificence.

> ***Who you are***
> ***makes***
> ***a***
> ***Magnificent difference***
> ***to the universe!***

Magnificent Affirmation
Praise

*Who I am
makes a Magnificent
difference!*

*Who you are
makes a Magnificent
difference!*

*This is
the joyous voice of Love
pouring its infinite praise
into the universe
of waiting
hearts*

*Every
expression of praise
that radiates from my life
fills my own being
with the light
of Love*

Loving Yourself with Magnificence!

Here is statement #21 again from the *Liberating Your Magnificence Quiz* in the appendix.

I praise others generously.

What are the three most powerful things you can do to align your life with this statement?

1. _____

   _____

   _____

2. _____

   _____

   _____

3. _____

   _____

   _____

It is
your
spiritual right
to be a
fountain of praise

Magnificence Journal

As you look into your own liberation, what are you discovering about your own habits of praising?

_____

_____

_____

_____

_____

_____

_____

_____

_____

_____

_____

_____

_____

_____

Chapter 22

Exude
Joy

Joy liberates and heals – gives light to the world!

Let joy burst into expression as the real you that says "Yes!" to liberation. How could Magnificence do less than radiate pure joy?

Joy is spiritual power! Each of us can affirm our oneness with joy itself:

- I affirm that joy is my natural state.
- My joy is like an endless well – inexhaustible.
- Nothing can keep me from joy today.
- I accept my nature as overflowing with joy.
- I can already envision myself expressing joy's constant Light.
- I'm going to look for the joyous side of everything that happens in my life today.
- I'm going to let myself laugh today to unite with my Magnificence.

***Joy
is the natural state
of Love
expressing
you***

Scott often walks past Shannon's closed door to her office and hears great bursts of laughter. It makes him smile and laugh even though he's not part of what's going on.

Her laughter reveals the healing power of joy. Many of the people calling Shannon for spiritual help are facing great life challenges with their health, marriages, businesses, and identities. Joy is good medicine.

Pure joy
lets in spiritual Light
that heals

We have learned to refuse any thought that says things are so bad that we can't access our joy. Even during the lawsuit that dominated the first years of our marriage, we found moments of great release in healing laughter.

We are also playful – every day. In fact, we have a whole series of playful joy-givers that giggle themselves through our lives.

For example, when we hold hands while sitting together, Shannon's thumb seems to always find its way on top of mine in our playful, gentle battle for thumb position.

Play & laughter
take us into
spiritual
Light

Even in disagreeing, we've learned the power of joy. We are both great believers of solving all problems through prayer, so sometimes – when one of us completely disagrees with the other's new idea or suggestion – we say, "Let's pray about that."

This brings instant laughter to the surface –
because we both know that statement is the most
gracious, elegant, divine way of temporarily saying
"No" without any hard feelings. Who can argue
against prayer?

The satisfying thing about this response is that
we really do pray – and this answer provides
breathing room for a new idea to sink in.

Rather surprisingly, we often warm up to each
other's ideas as they are allowed to simmer in prayer
devoid of argument.

Joy liberates the Magnificence of Love

Joy is not something outside us. Joy is already
present within each of us – right now!

We are incapable of being separated from joy.
The thought that suggests that joy is "over there" or
"not here" or "somewhere in the future" is invalid
thinking and not part of a consciousness of
liberation.

Joy is not an emotion – temporary or limited.
Joy is a spiritual quality – infinite and eternal –
flowing through your entire identity.

Joy is often quiet, expressed in spiritual wonder
and inner satisfaction. This is the natural state of
joy – and therefore *your* natural state in oneness
with joy.

Your spirituality weds you to joy

Whenever joy seems absent in your life, always move swiftly to your spirituality. Affirm your oneness with divine Love. Let a smile open in your heart as you acknowledge that Love always includes joy.

Thoughts that suggest we are not at one with joy are a mental imposition on our happiness:

- I'm just not happy right now in my life.
- It's not a good time for me.
- There's too much overload.
- I don't know how to be joyful.
- What joy?
- I'm too miserable to even think of something so far away as joy.

We can choose to see these as *false thoughts* trying to gain domination in our consciousness.

Joy is always a choice!

Here's one moment when Shannon learned this lesson with her close girlfriend – Dessa.

––––––––––

Dessa is one of the funniest persons I have ever known and she's been my dear friend for twenty years.

Every time we get together, you can hear the laughter from outside the walls. We bring out the funny side of each other and always have. I adore her.

Well, one gorgeous California day we were sitting outside under an umbrella at a restaurant when she told me she had an announcement to make – she was moving away!

I'll never forget that moment. We'd been intimate buddies for fifteen years. She was only moving 100 miles away and I knew in my heart that, if the move was right for her, it must also be right for me. But I felt her move would drastically change my life.

I held back the tears. I managed to share her joy, but I was frightened. It felt like massive light and joy were leaving me. Did someone turn out the lights? It surely felt so. A feeling of depression pushed hard at me.

I combated my feelings by remembering that joy is spiritual so could never be temporary – or lost.

As I stayed in this thought that my joy was inherent and permanent, I began to feel a sense of divine comfort. By the time she left a few weeks later, I felt strong and even confident that I would not experience loss.

In the years since her departure, I have found joy expressing itself in a multitude of new ways in my life. This is the nature of true joy.

When we claim joy as inherent and permanent – not dependent on a person or circumstance – we will always see it expressed in an infinite number of new ways.

Because
joy
is spiritual
we can never be deprived
of its
presence

The
consciousness of Magnificence
looks out on life
with spiritual awareness
that joy is
infinite

Dessa and I are still very close. Any time there's something new and wonderful in my life, she's the first one I call. And she does the same with me. She's my forever friend. Every time we get together, the laughter continues as if we had never been apart.

In fact, I've asked myself what it is about her that turns on the joy and giggles for me. The answer to this question reveals a great deal about what brings joy forward in our lives:

- We have an unwritten, unspoken agreement that we want to have fun and laugh when we are together.
- We are completely open with each other – no pretenses or pride.
- We tease each other constantly – but always with extravagant love.
- We make fun of ourselves – endlessly.
- We are just plain slapstick goofy – letting our childlike natures sing.
- We are non-judgmental. Joy bursts into being when there is no judgment.

On the next page is one of Dessa's own poems that captures this spirit.

On My Watch

What fun it is to observe
no obligation to reserve
personal opinions about what I see,
comparing events to what's happened to me!

Appreciation of what I perceive,
lets me enjoy the moment to conceive
a peace that can dismiss some view
of what someone else ought to do.

How freeing it is not to judge
or give advice that ends in some grudge.
To watch with unbiased revelation
satisfies every life expectation.

Dessa Byrd Reed

Magnificence Affirmation
Joy

*Joy
is my inherent spiritual
nature*

*In my
oneness with Love
joy pours forth
with infinite
radiance*

*I am a
fountain
of joyful being*

*I am
the smile of
God*

Loving Yourself with Magnificence!

Here is statement #22 again from the *Liberating Your Magnificence Quiz* in the appendix.

I exude joy.

What are the three most powerful things you can do to align your life with this statement?

1. _____

   _____

   _____

2. _____

   _____

   _____

3. _____

   _____

   _____

*It is your
spiritual right
to exude
joy*

Magnificence Journal

How is joy expressing itself in the liberation of *your* Magnificence?

_____

_____

_____

_____

_____

_____

_____

_____

_____

_____

_____

_____

_____

_____

Chapter 23

Live in the Consciousness of Infinite Possibilities

Look at the phenomenal view!

Here we are, standing at the mountaintop of Magnificence.

Because we have climbed so high, we're now able to scan the universe in all directions.

> ***Just as
> the universe is expanding,
> so too is
> your Magnificence
> expanding – exponentially***

Infinite expansion is a natural state of spirituality – so it is natural for us now to remove all resistance to ever-expanding, infinite possibilities of good. Quantum possibilities!

Even when we think we've taken huge steps of progress, we need to stand back and open the boundaries of our thought to successive quantum leaps into infinity.

Look at the brief history of travel on our planet –
from horse, to car, to propeller plane, to jet, to space
travel, to transmitting our communications by light!

We did not just *progress* to faster speeds. We
vaulted to greater speeds. The curve of ever-
increasing speeds in our short history is exponential.

Each time we leaped forward, it was because
someone decided that the next step was possible.

Let us *expect* such quantum leaps in our
personal lives!

> *When*
> *we admit*
> *that infinite good*
> *is possible*
> *we open our lives*
> *to*
> *exponential possibilities*

Your Magnificence is already liberated. The only
possible results now will be phenomenal advances in
your life. The *substance* of who you are cannot be
contained. Your unique Life Message includes within
itself infinite possibilities of expression.

So often we focus tightly on the *forms* – how our
substance will next be expressed, rearranging our
forms, or trying to create or preserve them – that we
lose sight of our *substance*.

Take your vision off *form.*

Let your *substance* soar to infinite possibilities.

Your true *substance* will be expanding into new
forms – for eternity. Let it happen! Enjoy it!

Think of yourself as watching and enjoying an
adventure movie called "Your Own Exponential Life
of Magnificence."

Let your true *substance* – your Magnificence – create its own *forms*. Let your spiritual passion – your Life Message – direct your life.

Don't even try to hold on to the current *forms* of your life. It's no longer possible. The liberation of your Magnificence is unstoppable and infinite.

Watch it go!

> **When you want
> to expand to
> full Magnificence,
> go deeper into your substance,
> not your form**

Here is a great exercise that shows the power of unrestricted Magnificence. Write below the highest idea of Magnificence that you can imagine for your life.

The highest idea of Magnificence I can imagine for my life right now is:

> **Your Magnificence
> can rise no higher than
> what you conceive
> as possible**

Now, think of yourself as infinite Mind, totally unrestricted in achieving all possibilities.

If divine Mind read the words you just wrote and wanted to advance you a quantum leap forward, what would Mind say was possible? Go ahead, think *as* Mind loving and expressing you with infinite possibility.

Mind's quantum leap beyond what I wrote would be:

Mind's view of your Magnificence is infinite

To open consciousness and think out from infinite possibilities, we need to unite with divine Mind, the intelligent Consciousness of all being.

Think of yourself right now as being at one with Mind. Divine Mind would not be saying:

- This part of me is Magnificent but this other part over there is not.
- This part of me is stuck and that part over there is running out of supply.
- If only I had more good I would be happier.

Mind is in a perpetual state of fulfillment. Its every desire is simultaneously fulfilled. Infinite desires – all fulfilled. Divine Mind does not look to anything outside of its all-inclusive wholeness. This is Mind's picture of infinite possibilities.

And this is *your* picture – because you are Mind's expression. This is your spiritual consciousness. This is home. Find your comfort here. Stay open to even more good.

The liberation of your Magnificence will always be continuous and exponential

Shannon often sits in her office thinking about infinity and looking out from its vastness. This is a vital part of her healing practice. Let her lead you in practicing "infinity thinking" right now. Here are her words:

———

Think of yourself – right now – as the consciousness of divine Mind, embodying all infinite, Magnificent spiritual qualities.

Now look out from this divine Consciousness and see the immense display of ideas.

Each idea is brilliant with beauty, intelligence, ability, might, power, rhythm, purpose, communication, attraction, union, discovery, fulfillment, multiplication, expansion, spontaneity, regeneration, and joy.

Think of all the ideas contained within infinite Consciousness – your consciousness as Mind's expression:

- Each idea is in a continual state of creative unfoldment.

- Each idea is eternal.
- Each idea expresses perfection.
- Each idea is perfectly integrated with all other ideas.
- All the ideas are immeasurable, without boundary, and simultaneously active.

This is a picture of infinite life. Divine Mind does not get exhausted at five o'clock. Mind – and you in oneness with Mind – does not get stressed over too much to do or too little time to accomplish it.

This is how Mind's reality looks. And this is *your* reality.

And there's more.

Mind never stops creating ideas – infinitely! And each new idea – and you include all of them – is unfolding with originality and freshness every divine moment, never to be duplicated.

Mind's ideas
by their very nature
have infinite substance and can never be
limited or contained

Each divine idea is super abundant, full of love, and is perfectly orchestrated. Not one of these ideas is asking:

- When will I get to my dreams?
- Will I ever be able to express what I came to do?
- I'm running out of time, money, and ideas. When will I get supplied?
- I'm too old. How can I stay fresh?

Each of us is the consciousness of timeless, ageless, deathless being. Each of us includes all ideas in infinity at once. And we include their harmonious interaction. This is our true self.

Magnificence consciousness never departs from its oneness with divine Mind

What must we do in order to experience this *all* the time?

Practice releasing all thoughts which bind – all thoughts which say, "I am finite."

In fact, here is the rule of Magnificent consciousness: If a finite or limited *thought* tries to enter your consciousness, the answer is "No!"

For example, the following thoughts would never make it into Magnificence consciousness:

- This is too good to be true.
- I don't deserve it.
- No one will help me.
- It probably won't happen
- It may be too late.

Magnificence consciousness affirms – with joy and dominion:

- I deserve all good.
- Yes, it's good enough to be true.
- My dreams are unfolding right now.
- The timing is perfect.
- I know that I am being supported by the Universe.

Infinity is your true nature. In Magnificence consciousness – the consciousness of infinite possibilities of good – we are all engaged in:

- Blessing each other.
- Praising each other.
- Seeing each other's Magnificence.

- Liberating each other.
- Expressing love.
- Esteeming each other.
- Singing, adoring, inspiring.

Let us never look back on our lives and feel that our dreams were too small. Or that we failed to dream. Or that we failed to unite with divine, infinite Mind.

Let your legacy be that you opened your life to the consciousness of infinite possibilities, accepted your oneness with infinite Mind, and rose to Magnificence consciousness.

> *Liberating your Magnificence*
> *is not a dream or hope.*
> *It is your*
> *inherent, spiritual*
> *right!*

As Diana Loomans, our good friend and talented author of *Full Esteem Ahead,* says so beautifully in her poem on the next page – dare to dream!

Dare to Dream!

I can no longer live a half-hearted life;
doubting my deepest desires,
hesitant to follow my dreams,
or afraid to discover my greatness.

I may have an endless stream of questions;
Am I worthy? Will I fail?
Do I have what it takes?
Will I be left alone, and with nothing?

The truth is, this can only happen
if I don't follow my dreams.
For what is more distressing than a dream
that might have been?
What causes more regret than the sorrow
of never having risked?
And what could be lonelier than living the
life of somebody else?

I was born to move boldly towards my
highest dreams,
Bring my most cherished desires to life.
There is a voice inside of me that proclaims;
I am here to express who I really am!
I am here to love and be loved!
I am here to be fully alive!
I am here to make a difference in this world!

I will wait no longer.
Have I forgotten that my deepest dreams arise
From a Great Source within me that longs
to fulfill them?
Remembering this, I leap courageously
into the unknown with faith;
Bringing my dreams to life, and inspiring
others to do the same.

Diana Loomans © 1999

Magnificence Affirmation
Infinite Possibilities

*I am at one
with Mind's
infinite expression*

*I am open
to infinite possibilities of good
and I live in the
consciousness of Magnificence*

*I understand
that the expectation and fulfillment
of all possibilities of good
is my natural state*

*All possibilities of Magnificence
are unfolding
before me
and all mankind*

Loving Yourself with Magnificence!

Here is statement #23 again from the *Liberating Your Magnificence Quiz* in the appendix.

I live in the consciousness of infinite possibilities.

What are the three most powerful things you can do to align your life with this statement?

1. _____

   _____

   _____

2. _____

   _____

   _____

3. _____

   _____

   _____

*It is your
spiritual right
to experience
infinite possibilities*

Magnificence Journal

How is your consciousness expanding to embrace infinite possibilities in the liberation of your Magnificence?

_____

_____

_____

_____

_____

_____

_____

_____

_____

_____

_____

_____

_____

_____

Chapter 24

Love
Unconditionally
&
Universally

Imagine arriving at the final door to the complete liberation of your Magnificence.

What would that door be labeled?

"Infinite Love"

Of course!

There is nothing higher than Love.

Think of how good we have all felt when we've seen the inspiring bumper sticker:

> "Practice random acts
> of kindness."

Now let's take love even higher.

Magnificence calls for us to practice *perpetual* acts of unconditional, universal love. This is the new threshold of love. The liberation of your Magnificence has brought you here – face to face with unconditional and universal Love.

Without Love, you cannot be Magnificent.

Magnificence
opens us to
Love

Love
opens us to
Magnificence

Magnificence and Love
are one

Here, at the peak of living in oneness with your Magnificence, you receive the greatest gift of all life – the opportunity to radiate infinite Love.

The voice of Magnificence speaks to us:

Practice
unconditional & universal
Love

And it's so easy. Here is an example from Scott's life – in his words:

———

I remember driving from Los Angeles to San Francisco through California's central valley one day. I took the long drive alone to have time to think about my Life Message and this book.

When I stopped at Denny's, there was a crowd – so I sat at the counter. I intended to quickly order a grilled cheese sandwich and be on my way, but something else happened.

A waitress appeared whom I had never met, but her name badge said "Suzie." She looked sad and my heart immediately went out to her. I looked her directly in the eyes and said: "Suzie, what's the most significant thing going on in your life right now?" Those were the first words of our conversation.

She looked at me with surprise and said, "Do you really want to know?"

"I sure do," I said, feeling totally at ease with being Love's expression.

Suzie reached for her order book, folded back the tickets and showed me a picture of her beautiful young daughter.

"This is my daughter. She's sixteen months old. She's the love of my life and I'm doing the best I can to raise her."

I was so touched by her openness that I told her I had a gift for her. I went to the car, grabbed a copy of our book, *The Love You Deserve*, and signed it to Suzie and her daughter. She accepted it with a smile and tears.

I still didn't have my grilled cheese sandwich, but that wasn't the end of the story. Within minutes, the manager came up to me and said, "Suzie showed me your book. Last night I got engaged. Can I buy a copy?"

Back to the trunk of the car. This is not why I stopped at Denny's! But when is the right time to love?

When is not the right time to love?

Imagine if I had entered Denny's with an attitude of anger or frustration at something going on in my life. Would that conversation with Suzie have occurred? Of course not! And so we learn an enormous lesson about Love and Magnificence:

The consciousness of perfect love precedes the experience

Think of all the people right now who need love:

- Women living in abuse and subordination.
- Young male teenagers in third world countries fighting futile wars.
- Homeless children living in the streets.
- Refugees without loved ones or homes.
- Elderly people who are poor and alone.
- Children abused, neglected, or abandoned.
- All who are victims of hate or injustice.
- Those struggling with health challenges.

All these people have a right to the liberation of their Magnificence. They deserve our love. They need our love. Is anything – ultimately – more powerful or liberating than Love?

Nothing!

Divine Love is really the word that best describes God – for Love inherently includes honoring, justice, principle, kindness, fairness, forgiveness, honesty, compassion, freedom, and equality. These are all words of liberation!

Liberation, Love, and Magnificence.

They come as one package. They are indivisible. They are you. They are all mankind. More love is the answer to every problem – and the answer to everyone's liberation.

Since the two of us are often referred to as "The Love Team," people often ask what goes on inside our thinking that makes our extraordinary relationship possible. If you could walk into our consciousness, this is what you would see:

- A deep commitment to living life in oneness – in complete unity – with divine Love.

- Dedication to practicing divine Love as our nature and seeing this as our inherent spiritual *right*.
- Determination to recover from mistakes through the power of forgiveness, gentle honesty, and unconditional Love.
- Anchoring of our consciousness in the knowledge that divine Love is the only real, permanent, and satisfying solution to any problem or condition in life – universally, for all mankind.
- Consistent prayer to align our thinking with divine Love and include all mankind in this healing Love.

This is the new consciousness of Love enveloping us all. This is mankind's true home.

***Love
is the
universal song
that unites and heals
all mankind***

Magnificence Affirmation

Unconditional
Universal
Love

*I rise
to the consciousness of
unconditional, universal Love
because I am
at one
with Love's Magnificence*

*I radiate
unconditional, universal Love
because divine Love
is
my true nature & identity*

*I embrace
all mankind
in
unconditional, universal Love
and affirm this Love
as our universal spiritual
right*

Loving Yourself with Magnificence!

Here is statement #24 again from the *Liberating Your Magnificence Quiz* in the appendix.

I love unconditionally and universally.

What are the three most powerful things you can do to align your life with this statement?

1. _____

   _____

   _____

2. _____

   _____

   _____

3. _____

   _____

   _____

It is your
spiritual right
to
radiate love
unconditionally and universally

Magnificence Journal

What are you discovering about radiating unconditional and universal love in your life?

_____

_____

_____

_____

_____

_____

_____

_____

_____

_____

_____

_____

_____

Chapter 25

Be a
Liberator!

You are a liberator!

You are here, at this page, because you have chosen liberation for your life.

- Look how much your consciousness has shifted in reading this book.
- Think of how far the liberation of your Magnificence has progressed.

Imagine the power of this liberation taking place in everyone you know!

And so you arrive at the end of this book to discover the glorious beginning – you now must teach and liberate others.

Nothing will boost your own progress faster than helping to liberate another person's Magnificence.

> *The*
> *mentor*
> *always learns*
> *more*
> *than the student*

You cannot change another person.

But you *can* present the environment, the love, the encouragement, and the tools for liberation to occur. That's all we've done for you.

Think of your best friend, your closest loved one, your spouse, daughter, son, father, mother, brother, sister, co-workers, and on and on.

- Are they in touch with their Magnificence?
- Is their Magnificence liberated?
- What secret dreams are still hidden within their private hearts?
- What do they yearn to be?
- When will they receive the opportunity?
- Who is teaching them?
- Who is loving them?

And think of all the people on Earth who are struggling for survival, physically and emotionally.

Who is reaching out to them?

You have reached a decisive turning point in your expanding life.

> *You simply cannot*
> *liberate your Magnificence*
> *without*
> *simultaneously*
> *liberating all mankind*

And so the only question that emerges at the mountaintop of Magnificence is:

> "How do I become an expert
> liberator myself?"

You begin with enormous humility.

- The first task is to liberate your own Magnificence as the expression of Soul.
- The second task is to make yourself available as an instrument of divine Love

– to be guided and used in Love's way –
to liberate others.

When those you yearn to help do not respond, let Love wash away the hurt and rejection, and let this be a proving ground for testing your unconditional and universal love.

***When
the student
is ready
the teacher will appear***

***So too, when
the teacher
is ready
the student will appear***

Seeking to be a liberator is not the answer.

Being a liberator is what opens us to healing opportunities.

A liberator remembers that the solution is always *within* the other person. The highest teacher creates an environment of unconditional love where another person can *experience* Love and discover Truth.

The consciousness of a liberator is anchored in universal equality – a total awareness there is no difference between gender, race, or religion. We are all spiritual beings and by that very definition, we are all equal in the eyes of Love.

Those who are led by Love to learn from you will *feel* your consciousness of equality. They will *feel* your expression of universal and unconditional love giving them freedom to accept only what serves their highest needs.

Let your life
***be a* demonstration**
of liberation and Magnificence,
not a sermon

And so we learn that to rise to the consciousness of being a liberator, is most humbling – because it literally *forces* us to *be* what we profess.

We become the liberated!

As you now arrive at the end of this book, think of yourself as joining hands with everyone else reading this book – in a universal circle of love – cherishing each other as equals, standing ready to defend each other, each of us radiating our Magnificence in a bond of living love embracing all mankind.

Thank you for joining hands with us.

Your life mission
is to liberate your inner substance
– your unique Magnificence –
to bless the universe
with what you
alone are

And
on the way
to love and honor and liberate
the Magnificence
of all those you pass and know

Magnificence Affirmation
Liberating all mankind

*I understand
that the liberation of all mankind
is also
my liberation*

*I affirm
my oneness with divine Love
that empowers me
to radiate
all-inclusive, all-liberating
divine Love*

*I affirm
all mankind's spiritual right
to experience complete
liberation
of
Magnificence*

Loving Yourself with Magnificence!

Here is statement #25 again from the *Liberating Your Magnificence Quiz* in the appendix.

I am actively engaged in liberating Magnificence within others.

What are the three most powerful things you can do to align your life with this statement?

1. _____

   _____

   _____

2. _____

   _____

   _____

3. _____

   _____

   _____

It is your
spiritual right
to be a
liberator of Magnificence
for all mankind

Magnificence Journal

How has this book affected your life and the liberation of your Magnificence?

_____

_____

_____

_____

_____

_____

_____

_____

_____

_____

_____

_____

_____

_____

Appendix

Quiz:
How Liberated
is Your Magnificence?

Circle a number for each statement. Each question corresponds to the same-numbered chapter in the book.

Stage 1
Identify Your Magnificence

1. I am open to the Magnificence within me.

    1 2 3 4 5 6 7 8 9 10
    Not at all   Somewhat   Completely

2. I understand that my Magnificence is the *substance* of who I am, not the *form* of my life *(job, title, role)*.

    1 2 3 4 5 6 7 8 9 10
    Not at all   Somewhat   Completely

3. I am able to identify my unique Life Message in one sentence.

    1 2 3 4 5 6 7 8 9 10
    Not at all   Somewhat   Completely

Continued on next page

Stage 2
Cherish Your Magnificence

4.   I give myself sacred solitude to nurture and cherish my Magnificence.

   1   2   3   4   5   6   7   8   9   10
   Not at all   Somewhat   Completely

5.   I see myself as *already* whole, not incomplete.

   1   2   3   4   5   6   7   8   9   10
   Not at all   Somewhat   Completely

6.   I refuse to compare myself with others.

   1   2   3   4   5   6   7   8   9   10
   Not at all   Somewhat   Completely

7.   I surround myself with people who cherish, honor, esteem, and empower me.

   1   2   3   4   5   6   7   8   9   10
   Not at all   Somewhat   Completely

8.   I welcome expansion in my life.

   1   2   3   4   5   6   7   8   9   10
   Not at all   Somewhat   Completely

9.   I live fully in the present moment, not in the past or future.

   1   2   3   4   5   6   7   8   9   10
   Not at all   Somewhat   Completely

10. I trust the power of Love to liberate my Magnificence.

    1   2   3   4   5   6   7   8   9   10
    Not at all   Somewhat   Completely

11. I am an expert at making spiritual affirmations.

    1   2   3   4   5   6   7   8   9   10
    Not at all   Somewhat   Completely

Stage 3
Free Your Magnificence

12. I live in the freedom of Soul rather than in the dungeon of doubt.

    1   2   3   4   5   6   7   8   9   10
    Not at all   Somewhat   Completely

13. I live without guilt.

    1   2   3   4   5   6   7   8   9   10
    Not at all   Somewhat   Completely

14. I live in the consciousness of abundance, not lack.

    1   2   3   4   5   6   7   8   9   10
    Not at all   Somewhat   Completely

15. I live without fear in the assurance of divine Love.

    1   2   3   4   5   6   7   8   9   10
    Not at all   Somewhat   Completely

16. I live in the consciousness of Love that dissolves all anger.

    1 2 3 4 5 6 7 8 9 10
Not at all   Somewhat   Completely

17. I live outside of time and age in eternity consciousness.

    1 2 3 4 5 6 7 8 9 10
Not at all   Somewhat   Completely

18. I quickly move past rejection to a higher unfoldment of Magnificence.

    1 2 3 4 5 6 7 8 9 10
Not at all   Somewhat   Completely

19. I shift swiftly from overwhelm to liberation.

    1 2 3 4 5 6 7 8 9 10
Not at all   Somewhat   Completely

Stage 4
Radiate Your Magnificence

20. I take one step every day to liberate my Magnificence.

    1 2 3 4 5 6 7 8 9 10
Not at all   Somewhat   Completely

21. I praise others generously.

    1 2 3 4 5 6 7 8 9 10
Not at all   Somewhat   Completely

22. I exude joy.

1 2 3 4 5 6 7 8 9 10
Not at all   Somewhat   Completely

23. I live in the consciousness of infinite possibilities.

1 2 3 4 5 6 7 8 9 10
Not at all   Somewhat   Completely

24. I love unconditionally & universally.

1 2 3 4 5 6 7 8 9 10
Not at all   Somewhat   Completely

25. I am actively engaged in liberating Magnificence within others.

1 2 3 4 5 6 7 8 9 10
Not at all   Somewhat   Completely

Rating
on next page

Rating:
How Liberated
is Your Magnificence?

Total score: _____ divided by 25 = _____

1-2   Hidden Magnificence. Your Magnificence may seem to be hidden, but this is not so. You are being called out of darkness by Love. Let Love lead you to the Light that transforms and heals. This is your spiritual *right*.

3-4   Glimpsing your Magnificence. Your Magnificence is calling for more Light so that it may shine with greater clarity in your own consciousness. Open yourself to all Light.

5-6   Cherishing your Magnificence. Your Magnificence is already shining and you can feel the benefits. Let your Magnificence rise into free and radiating completeness.

7-8   Freeing your Magnificence. You have worked hard to free your Magnificence. Your contribution to others – and the universe – is immense. Let yourself break into pure Light.

9-10   Radiating your Magnificence! Your Magnificence is radiating with healing power to everyone around you and out to the entire universe. You have become a liberator of mankind's Magnificence!

About the Authors

Scott & Shannon Peck are co-founders of *TheLoveCenter™*, a non-profit corporation dedicated to bringing all mankind into the heart of Love. They speak and give workshops on *The Love You Deserve* and *Liberating Your Magnificence* as well as other topics.

Scott has served as a reporter, educator, counselor, advertising manager, real estate broker, author, and speaker. He holds a Master's Degree in Education.

Shannon has been a spiritual healer since 1981 and has also served as a TV talk show host, prison chaplain, author, and speaker.

The Pecks live in San Diego, California.

Your Response is Welcome

Many have reported transformations and healings from reading this book. If this book has had a significant impact on you, we'd love to hear from you. Please tell us your story.

E-mail:
PeckMsg@AOL.com

Scott & Shannon Peck
TheLoveCenter™
P. O. Box 830
Solana Beach, CA 92075

The Love You Deserve

Liberating Your Magnificence is a companion to the widely-acclaimed first book, **The Love You Deserve:10 Keys to Perfect Love**, also available at bookstores.

Please visit

If you'd like to know more about us or *TheLoveCenter*™, please visit our website:

TheLoveCenter.com